Vocabulary, Reading, and Writing Exercises

SAT™ POWER PREP

SECOND EDITION

Project Editor:
Daniel Reed

Production Editor:
Darlene Gilmore

Senior Editor:
Paul Moliken

Contributors:
Rachel Natbony
Lisa Tetrault
Leah Rodriguez
Sydney Palmer
Allison Billmire
Alana Domingo

Cover Design:
Chris Koniencki

 Printed in the United States of America. *2nd Edition 2018*

ISBN: 978-1-62019-368-6

Vocabulary, Reading, and Writing Exercises

OVERVIEW:

2 Full-length **SAT** Reading and Writing and Language practice tests with vocabulary instruction

2 Units divided into 20 lessons

54 Contextual vocabulary exercises based on vocabulary used in the **SAT**-style practice passages

18 Grammar for writing exercises to prepare for the **SAT** writing test

Writing prompts and scoring guides for **SAT** essay practice

Table of Contents

Unit 1

Unit 2

Reading Test

Each passage or pair of passages, some of which are accompanied by graphics such as maps, charts, or graphs, is followed by a set of questions. Read the passage and then choose the best answer to each of the questions.

UNIT ONE

Lesson 1

Questions 1–10 are based on the following passage.

This passage is adapted from Fyodor Dostoyevsky's *The Idiot*, published 1869, translated 1915.

But for all this, the question remains,—what are the novelists to do with commonplace people, and how are they to be presented to the reader in such a form as to be in the least degree interesting? They cannot be left out altogether, for commonplace people meet one at every turn of life, and to leave them out would be to destroy the whole reality and probability of the story. To fill a novel with typical characters only, or with merely strange and uncommon people, would render the book unreal and improbable, and would very likely destroy the interest. In my opinion, the duty of the novelist is to seek out points of interest and instruction even in the characters of commonplace people.

For instance, when the whole essence of an ordinary person's nature lies in his **perpetual** and unchangeable commonplaceness; and when in spite of all his endeavors to do something out of the common, this person ends, eventually, by remaining in his unbroken line of routine. I think such an individual really does become a type of his own—a type of commonplaceness which will not for the world, if it can help it, be **contented**, but strains and **yearns** to be something original and independent, without the slightest possibility of being so. To this class of commonplace people belong several characters in this novel;—characters which—I admit—I have not drawn very vividly up to now for my reader's benefit.

Such were, for instance, Varvara Ardalionovna Ptitsin, her husband, and her brother, Gania.

There is nothing so annoying as to be fairly rich, of a fairly good family, pleasing presence, average education, to be "not stupid," kind-hearted, and yet to have no talent at all, no originality, not a single idea of one's own—to be, in fact, "just like everyone else."

Of such people there are countless numbers in this world—far more even than appear. They can be divided into two classes as all men can—that is, those of limited intellect, and those who are much cleverer. The former of these classes is the happier.

To a commonplace man of limited intellect, for instance, nothing is simpler than to imagine himself an original character, and to revel in that belief without the slightest misgiving.

Many of our young women have thought fit to cut their hair short, put on blue spectacles and call themselves **Nihilists**. By doing this they have been able to persuade themselves, without further trouble, that they have acquired new **convictions** of their own. Some men have but felt some little **qualm** of kindness towards their fellow-men, and the fact has been quite enough to persuade them that they stand alone in the van of enlightenment and that no one has such humanitarian feelings as they. Others have but to read an idea of somebody else's, and they can immediately **assimilate** it and believe that it was a child of their own brain. The "**impudence** of ignorance," if I may use the expression, is developed to a wonderful extent in such cases;—unlikely as it appears, it is met with at every turn.

This confidence of a stupid man in his own talents has been wonderfully depicted by Gogol in the amazing character of Pirogoff. Pirogoff has not the slightest doubt of his own genius,—nay, of his superiority of genius,—so certain is he of it that he never questions it. How

Lesson 1 continued:

many Pirogoffs have there not been among our writers—scholars, **propagandists**?

I say "have been," but indeed there are plenty of them at this very day.

Our friend, Gania, belonged to the other class—to the "much cleverer" persons, though he was from head to foot **permeated** and saturated with the longing to be original. This class, as I have said above, is far less happy. For the "clever commonplace" person, though he may possibly imagine himself a man of genius and originality, nonetheless has within his heart the deathless worm of suspicion and doubt; and this doubt sometimes brings a clever man to despair. (As a rule, however, nothing tragic happens;—his liver becomes a little damaged in the course of time, nothing more serious. Such men do not give up their **aspirations** after originality without a severe struggle,—and there have been men who, though good fellows in themselves, and even benefactors to humanity, have sunk to the level of **base** criminals for the sake of originality).

Gania was a beginner, as it were, upon this road. A deep and unchangeable consciousness of his own lack of talent, combined with a vast longing to be able to persuade himself that he was original, had **rankled** in his heart, even from childhood.

He seemed to have been born with **overwrought** nerves, and in his passionate desire to excel, he was often led to the brink of some rash step; and yet, having resolved upon such a step, when the moment arrived, he invariably proved too sensible to take it. He was ready, in the same way, to do a base action in order to obtain his wished-for object; and yet, when the moment came to do it, he found that he was too honest for any great baseness. (Not that he objected to acts of petty meanness—he was always ready for them.) He looked with hate and loathing on the poverty and downfall of his family, and treated his mother with **haughty** contempt, although he knew that his whole future depended on her character and reputation.

1

Choose the answer that best describes the purpose of this passage.

A) an argument against plain characters
B) commentary on Nihilists
C) writing advice from an author
D) an analysis of Pirogoff's morality

2

Which phrase from the passage provides the best evidence for your answer to the previous question?

A) Lines 11-13 ("In my opinion…people")
B) Lines 14-18 ("For instance…routine")
C) Lines 23-26 ("To this…benefit")
D) Lines 39-42 ("To a commonplace…misgiving")

3

In paragraph 1, the author implies that the traditional approach to portraying common people is to

A) ensure they are especially unremarkable.
B) make the boring characters interesting.
C) use common characters for main characters.
D) keep the boring character scenes to a minimum.

4

According to paragraph 2, the trait that makes a common person (character) most interesting is

A) the character's ultimate success.
B) that character's inability to change.
C) the knowledge that he or she can change.
D) knowing that he or she will never change.

Lesson 1 continued:

5

The author suggests that "commonplace" people can be divided into two classes, and that the happier class can be described as having

A) more opportunities than the other has.
B) everything handed to it.
C) reasons for maintaining the status quo.
D) less intelligence than the other has.

6

Choose the statement most closely paraphrases the sentence in lines 39-42 ("To a…misgiving").

A) People of limited intellect are frustrated by it.
B) Ignorance is bliss.
C) The simple solution is usually the correct one.
D) Intellectuals have easier lives.

7

The author suggests that there are three classifications of people of "limited intellect." Choose the answer that is *not* one of the three classifications.

A) those who become experts in a subject
B) those who simply copy the beliefs of others
C) those whose common feelings lead them to believe they are unique
D) those who pretend to be something and then begin to believe it

8

As it is used in line 74, *deathless* suggests that a clever person's despair is

A) tolerable.
B) amplified.
C) permanent.
D) ancient.

9

As it is used in line 82, the word *base* most nearly means

A) remarkable.
B) bitter.
C) questionable.
D) evil.

10

The author of the passage would agree with which one of the following statements?

A) To create a boring character, simply delve deeper into a character's personality.
B) There's no such thing as an uninteresting person.
C) The most uninteresting character is one smart enough to know that he or she is not special.
D) The best novels are filled with strange, uncommon characters.

Lesson 1 continued:

Vocabulary: Context Answers

The following sentences contain vocabulary words used in the reading passage. Choose the answer that best completes the sentence. There may be more than one technically correct answer, but one will better exemplify the italicized vocabulary word than the others will.

1) Fish that swim _____ live in *perpetual* darkness.
   A. underneath fishing piers
   B. in the deepest trenches of the ocean
   C. in the Pacific Ocean
   D. around the perimeter of coral reefs
   E. in the kelp forests of Southern California

2) _____, Emily gave a *contented* sigh.
   A. After scheduling her dentist appointment
   B. Standing outside in the drizzle
   C. Reclining by the hotel's pool
   D. Before starting her speech
   E. Looking through the jewelry store window

3) Walter *yearns* _____ as he sits in the dreary waiting room.
   A. because of the crying child
   B. on the cushioned bench
   C. that the doctor is late
   D. for the summer breeze
   E. yet does not complain

4) The judge believes _____ does not align with his moral *convictions*.
   A. telling the truth
   B. running for mayor
   C. accepting bribes
   D. donating to local charities
   E. taking a day off

5) _____, Ben has no *qualms* about copying his friend's essay.
   A. Afraid of failing the class
   B. Under the guidance of his friends
   C. Even though his grades are satisfactory
   D. Although the paper is due next week
   E. Despite the threat of punishment

6) Because Heather _____, she needed to *assimilate*.
   A. received detention
   B. wanted good grades
   C. did not study for the math exam
   D. left her textbooks at home
   E. transferred to a new school

7) Roger spoke with *impudence*, his voice _____.
   A. shaking with fear
   B. defiant and strong
   C. quiet from embarrassment
   D. loud and uncertain
   E. stern and commanding

8) Rain from the heavy storm *permeated* _____.
   A. the hard soil
   B. the truck's roof
   C. my plastic umbrella
   D. the backyard deck
   E. the large lake

Lesson 1 continued:

9) Since Ricky _____, he has *aspirations* of becoming an actor.
   A. understands the basics of movie making
   B. has stage fright
   C. grew up watching movies
   D. did not get the leading role
   E. drove his friend to the audition

10) His actions were so *base* that _____.
   A. I refused to remain friends with him
   B. nobody seemed to notice
   C. he became exhausted
   D. he left us all confused
   E. we nominated him for office

11) Lori was clearly *overwrought* when she discovered _____.
   A. her pet cat was missing
   B. her brother was coming home for Thanksgiving
   C. her favorite team won the football tournament
   D. she forgot to do the laundry
   E. she was chosen as class president

12) Jackie's *haughty* remarks _____ her supervisor during the company meeting.
   A. amused
   B. irritated
   C. inspired
   D. helped
   E. informed

Lesson 1 continued:

Writing Practice

The underlined portion of each sentence possibly contains a flaw related to pronoun use. Select the answer that best corrects the flaw. Select NO CHANGE if the underlined portion is correct.

1) If anyone dislikes my music, <u>they can go</u> somewhere else.
   A. NO CHANGE
   B. they can goes
   C. he or she can go
   D. they go

2) The teacher said that either girl <u>could write her</u> answer on the board.
   A. NO CHANGE
   B. could write their
   C. can write their
   D. write her

3) We saw the stars on the badge and remembered that <u>each symbolize a precept of the organization</u>.
   A. NO CHANGE
   B. it each symbolizes a precept of the organization
   C. each symbolizes a precept of the organization
   D. each of the stars symbolize the organization's precept

4) Neither Janet nor Laurie <u>drives their</u> car to school.
   A. NO CHANGE
   B. drive her
   C. drive their
   D. drives her

5) Dad said that if anything is not returned to <u>their</u> proper place, we will be in trouble.
   A. NO CHANGE
   B. its
   C. everything's
   D. one's

6) Party planners praised the decorating committee because <u>it has worked</u> so hard.
   A. NO CHANGE
   B. they have worked
   C. they worked
   D. it have worked

7) Every tech company wants to retain <u>their</u> innovative employees.
   A. NO CHANGE
   B. its
   C. it's
   D. one's

8) Helena confided in her sister that something about their dad's actions <u>seem</u> off.
   A. NO CHANGE
   B. seems
   C. seem to be
   D. were seemingly

LANGUAGE
PRONOUNS 1

Lesson 1 continued:

9) When trekking through the desert, a hiker knows that they have to carry a lot of water to stay hydrated.
   A. NO CHANGE
   B. anybody has
   C. they need
   D. he or she has

10) People who notice the missing number in the puzzle receives a prize.
   A. NO CHANGE
   B. notice the missing numbers in the puzzles receives a prize.
   C. notice the missing number in the puzzle receive a prize.
   D. notices the missing number in the puzzle receives a prize.

Lesson 1 continued:

Vocabulary: Choosing the Right Use

The following sentences contain vocabulary words used in the reading passage. Identify the sentence or sentences that use the italicized vocabulary word properly. We have changed the form of some vocabulary words to provide new contexts; for example, some adjectives and verbs have been used as nouns.

1) A. In the weeks following his daughter's accident, Brandon was in a *perpetual* state of worry about her safety.
   B. The *perpetual* length of the speech allowed the spectators enough time to take photos of all the guest speakers afterwards.
   C. In the vacuum of space, absent of air to create friction, the planet will revolve around the sun *perpetually*.
   D. The *perpetual* snowstorm we had yesterday means that school will probably be in session today.

2) A. Trudy hoped her ripe and *contented* tomatoes would at least make her a finalist at the county fair competition.
   B. Even though he had really wanted the promotion, Jared remained *content* with his current position.
   C. The sun's rays shone *contentedly* through the clouds.
   D. After a long day, Janie *contented* herself with a bubble bath.

3) A. Although he tries to hide it, we all know that Tim *yearns* for a chance to play as the team's quarterback.
   B. Courtney takes the *yearning* back roads when she wants to go to Sarah's house.
   C. The door creaks loudly whenever it *yearns* open.
   D. The child cries whenever he is hungry or *yearns* for his mother.

4) A. Martin's *convictions* about standing up for himself faded immediately when he was caught off guard and forced to open the bank vault at gunpoint.
   B. After the autopsy, the coroner noted his *conviction* that the death was not accidental.
   C. Mary believes her neighbors have standing *convictions* against them, as they are very private people.
   D. Todd's *convictions* with the Florida summer season led him to buy a house in Alaska.

5) A. When the *qualm* between Jeff and Nick became physical, both of them were sent to the principal's office.
   B. The mechanic told me he would not be able to fix the *qualms* with my car until next week.
   C. Because Judy had proven herself able to handle stressful situations, her boss had no *qualms* about increasing her workload.
   D. The house looks good overall, but potential buyers may voice some *qualms* over the outdated electricity.

Lesson 1 continued:

6) A. Although Ted had never left his home country before, he had no problem *assimilating* into other cultures.
   B. If you want to do well in the class, you must *assimilate* to the course material.
   C. Jason thought he had copied Tara's homework secretly, but the teacher caught the *assimilation* right away.
   D. If you want to *assimilate* to a new lifestyle, it might be a good idea to do some research about it first.

7) A. Lily is a nice girl, but her *impudence* makes it difficult to trust her.
   B. Janis was fired from her job because of the *impudence* she showed her supervisors.
   C. Harry thought he could convince his guests to stay if he exhibited some *impudence*.
   D. Customers who behave with *impudence* will receive excellent service.

8) A. Because someone left the fog machine on all night, our house is in a *permeated* haze.
   B. The scent of the roses Jill's husband bought her *permeated* the room.
   C. When Tina found out her cookies won first place, she was *permeated* with joy.
   D. The teacher taught so well that her love for the subject *permeated* the entire class.

9) A. The suddenness of the deer in front of her car surprised Darla so much that she was still *rankled* long after she arrived home.
   B. When Bess arrived at work late and *rankled*, her boss called her into his office.
   C. *Rankled* by her noisy roommates, Lindsey closed her door and turned on her music.
   D. Because Joe had allowed his emotions to *rankle* inside him, he had become bitter and disagreeable.

10) A. Everyone could tell by Julie's continuous pacing before the award ceremony that she was *overwrought* with anxiety.
    B. The bride was *overwrought* when she realized she fit into her wedding dress.
    C. Investigators determined that the bridge had collapsed because it had been *overwrought* by rust.
    D. The three cups of coffee did nothing to help the prospective employee's *overwrought* nerves.

11) A. Sam's *haughty* attitude at the soup kitchen made her unpopular among the other volunteers.
    B. Ned's position as the school's star athlete made him popular, but his peers loved him even more for his *haughty* behavior.
    C. Her flirtatious but *haughty* expression sent mixed signals to all the guys at the party.
    D. An effective commercial for the ASPCA would have a famous, *haughty* celebrity who is holding a puppy.

Lesson 1 continued:

Synonyms and Antonyms

Match the word with its *antonym*.

1) perpetual	**A.** calm
2) content	**B.** politeness
3) yearn	**C.** short-lived
4) overwrought	**D.** modest
5) haughty	**E.** reject
6) impudence	**F.** displeased

Match the word with its *synonym*.

7) assimilate	**A.** misgiving
8) permeate	**B.** dream
9) rankle	**C.** pervade
10) qualm	**D.** integrate
11) conviction	**E.** anger
12) aspiration	**F.** judgment

END of LESSON 1

Lesson 2

Questions 11–20 are based on the following passage.

This passage is a summary of market trends in printed and electronic books.

With the invention of electronic book readers in the mid-2000s, publishers have been concerned that printed books could soon become **obsolete**; after all, e-readers are lightweight and can store hundreds of electronic works in a tiny, portable library. As people increasingly used technology, it seemed **plausible** to social scientists that readers might abandon traditional paper books.

For a while, e-readers certainly seemed to be the future. Between 2008 and 2010, electronic book sales rose a tremendous 1,260 percent to $1.6 billion. In 2011, twenty million devices were sold worldwide. Around that time, booksellers struggled to stay open, and one major bookstore chain, Borders, filed for **bankruptcy**; however, the initial rate of e-book sales did not last. By 2014, only twelve million e-readers were sold, down forty percent from three years previous. E-book sales also slowed and fell by ten percent in the first half of 2015. In comparison, the sales of print books fell by less than three percent in the same period. It appeared that the so-called "death of the printed book" would not come to pass, at least not anytime soon; in fact, there has been a **resurgence** of bookstores. The American Booksellers Association keeps track of independent bookstores across the United States. In 2015, the group had 1,712 member stores in 2,227 locations, up from 1,410 stores in 1,660 locations five years prior. A number of major publishing companies, including Hachette and Penguin Random House, have expanded their warehouses to **accommodate** more books.

Even young people, once **augured** to be the group most inclined to consume e-books, have unexpectedly **gravitated** toward paper books. In a 2013 poll, ninety-two percent of 18- to 29-year-olds reported reading print books. In another survey, almost half of 16- to 34-year-olds in the United States said that electronic books would not replace printed books for them. Printed books clearly have a lasting appeal that e-books lack. This appeal is likely due to the physical properties of printed books, from the illustrated covers to the **tactile** sensation of turning pages. These properties may also contribute to a greater retention of information; people, for whatever reason or combination of factors, can better **recollect** the contents of a printed book than those of an e-book. The printed word survives better than the digital in more ways than one.

The undying nature of printed books does not **inherently** mean that electronic books do not have a place in the book market. While e-books are not likely to replace their traditional counterparts, they do make up a significant share of the market. In the period between 2008 and 2013, US book sales rose eight percent to fifteen billion dollars, and e-book sales accounted for over three billion dollars. If e-books were removed from the total, however, book sales would be down eight percent; thus, e-book sales remain important for the overall economic health of the book market. Perhaps this statistic indicates that both media have their place in reading culture.

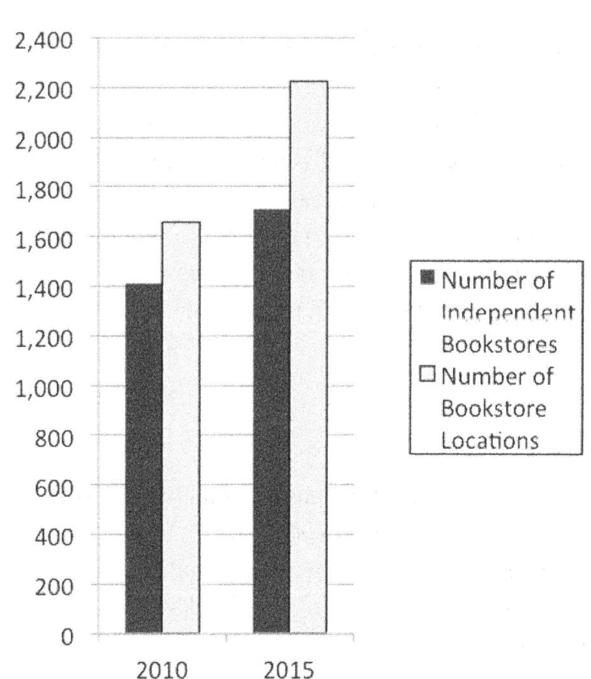

Lesson 2 continued:

11

Choose the most appropriate title for the passage.

A) The Future of the E-Book
B) Throw Away Your E-Book Reader
C) Effectiveness of Digital Products in Classrooms
D) The Fall and Rise of the Paper Book

12

The chart would seem to contradict which lines from the passage?

A) Lines 5-7 ("As people…books")
B) Lines 8-9 ("For a while…future")
C) Lines 11-14 ("Around…last")
D) Lines 19-22 ("It appeared…bookstores")

13

Paragraph 2 (lines 8-29) draws a distinction between which two types of booksellers?

A) independent sellers and online sellers
B) major chains and independent sellers
C) e-book distributors and major chains
D) Internet sellers and major chains

14

The author of the passage would probably agree with which one of the following statements?

A) Printed books have advantages over e-books.
B) E-books will definitely cause printed books to become obsolete, but not for a while.
C) Major chains will soon offer only e-books, and printed books will be special-order only.
D) The print industry will not recover from the loss in sales in 2010.

15

Choose the line from the passage that best supports your answer to the previous question.

A) Lines 22-24 ("The American…States")
B) Lines 30-32 ("Even young…books")
C) Lines 36-37 ("Printed books…lack")
D) Lines 34-36 ("In another…them")

16

Choose the line from paragraph 3 that could best be described as speculation or guessing.

A) Lines 34-36 ("In another…them")
B) Lines 40-43 ("These properties…e-book")
C) Lines 30-32 ("Even young…books")
D) Lines 36-37 ("Printed books…lack")

17

Identify the words or phrase that provides evidence that best supports your answer to the previous question.

A) "for whatever reason" (lines 41-42)
B) "lasting appeal" (line 37)
C) "tactile sensation" (line 39)
D) "In a 2013 poll" (line 32)

18

As it is used in line 30, *augured* most nearly means

A) dismissed.
B) unlikely.
C) condemned.
D) predicted.

19

Choose the word or phrase from the context of *augured* that best supports your answer to the previous question.

A) young people
B) paper books
C) inclined
D) unexpectedly

20

According to the graphic, in five years, the number of independent bookstores increased by

A) 50 businesses.
B) 300 businesses.
C) 1,200 businesses.
D) 3,300 businesses.

Lesson 2 continued:

Vocabulary: Context Answers

The following sentences contain vocabulary words used in the reading passage. Choose the answer that best completes the sentence. There may be more than one technically correct answer, but one will better exemplify the italicized vocabulary word than the others will.

1) _____ may soon make the operation of traditional cars *obsolete.*
   A. Alternative forms of fuel
   B. Improvements in highways
   C. Driverless cars
   D. Increased toll fees
   E. Space travel

2) Albert _____ because he gave a *plausible* excuse for his absence.
   A. fought with a coworker
   B. asked his manager for advice
   C. received a demotion
   D. was fired from his job
   E. was ultimately forgiven

3) After the holiday season, _____ drove the department store into *bankruptcy.*
   A. the closure of a competing company
   B. a drop in sales
   C. an abundance of new customers
   D. positive customer reviews
   E. a boost in the economy

4) The _____ created a *resurgence* of young families in the town.
   A. construction of a new elementary school
   B. closing of a daycare center
   C. introduction of several new restaurants
   D. opening of a new senior center
   E. announcement of a new highway system

5) The _____ could not *accommodate* all of the concertgoers.
   A. team of security guards
   B. popularity of the singer
   C. day of the performance
   D. limited number of seats
   E. theater's sound quality

6) The results of the laboratory tests *augured* that the patient _____.
   A. did not perform the tests correctly
   B. needed to take the tests earlier
   C. would not recover from his illness
   D. refused to receive treatment
   E. should have seen a doctor sooner

7) Although her parents wanted her to study medicine, Selena *gravitated* _____.
   A. against their wishes
   B. away from home
   C. upon seeing the cost of college
   D. toward world history
   E. and went to law school

8) The *tactile* exhibit at the history museum lets guests _____.
   A. purchase small souvenirs
   B. touch the bones of ancient dinosaurs
   C. learn about different types of cloth and materials
   D. see what life was like in ancient China
   E. feel a variety of emotions

Lesson 2 continued:

9) "Can you *recollect* _____?" asked the detective.
   A. next week's schedule
   B. any evidence from the crime scene
   C. the events from last night
   D. the insurance payments
   E. a probable cause

10) Marc believes all people are *inherently* _____ and that no person is born a criminal.
   A. misunderstood
   B. greedy
   C. poor
   D. selfless
   E. good

Lesson 2 continued:

Writing Practice

Each of the following sentences contains a modifying phrase that may or may not be clear or correct. Choose the answer that best corrects the sentence while retaining the intended meaning of the original sentence. Select NO CHANGE if the provided sentence is correct.

1) After playing in the snow, the bowl of soup was eaten by the cold child.
   A. NO CHANGE
   B. The child ate a bowl of cold soup after playing in the snow.
   C. The cold child ate a bowl of soup after playing in the snow.
   D. After playing in the snow, the cold child ate a bowl of soup.

2) Confirming our emails, the scuba gear will be shipped by tomorrow at noon.
   A. NO CHANGE
   B. I am confirming our emails, and the scuba gear will be shipped by tomorrow at noon.
   C. While confirming our emails, the scuba gear will be shipped by tomorrow at noon.
   D. The scuba gear will be shipped by tomorrow at noon, confirming our emails.

3) By being careful and hanging up the towel, this entire mess could have been avoided.
   A. NO CHANGE
   B. To avoid this entire mess, be careful and hang up the towel.
   C. While being careful and hanging up the towel, I could have avoided this entire mess.
   D. I could have avoided this entire mess by being careful and hanging up the towel.

4) Climbing slowly across the sky until noon, the heat of the sun burned the settlers.
   A. NO CHANGE
   B. The heat of the sun, climbing slowly across the sky until noon, burned the settlers.
   C. The sun, climbing slowly across the sky until noon, burned the settlers.
   D. The sun climbing slowly across the sky until noon, the heat burned the settlers.

5) While being taught how to fish, I knew I had hooked a bass because my rod suddenly bent.
   A. NO CHANGE
   B. Being taught how to fish, my rod suddenly bent, and I knew I had hooked a bass.
   C. Because my rod suddenly bent while being taught how to fish, I knew I had hooked a bass.
   D. I knew I had hooked a bass because my rod suddenly bent while being taught how to fish.

6) Left all alone in the house, some thunder frightened Ethan.
   A. NO CHANGE
   B. Left all alone in his house, Ethan became frightened by the thunder.
   C. Ethan, who had been left all alone in his house, the thunder frightened him.
   D. Some thunder frightened Ethan, left all alone in the house.

Lesson 2 continued:

7) Kissing my wife goodbye, the car was ready for me.
   A. NO CHANGE
   B. The car was ready for me after kissing my wife goodbye.
   C. When kissing my wife goodbye, the car was ready for me.
   D. After kissing my wife goodbye, I saw the car was ready for me.

8) Waiting for the timer to start, the stove began to heat up.
   A. NO CHANGE
   B. Waiting for the timer to start, the heating up of the stove began.
   C. As I was waiting for the timer to start, the stove began to heat up.
   D. The stove began to heat up while it was waiting for the timer to start.

9) To become successful, good planning is one of the first steps to take.
   A. NO CHANGE
   B. To become successful, one of the first steps to take is good planning.
   C. Good planning to become successful is one of the first steps for you to take.
   D. Good planning is one of the first steps to take in order to become successful.

10) Paved recently, the driver avoided 4th Street.
   A. NO CHANGE
   B. Because it was paved recently, the driver avoided 4th Street.
   C. Paving it recently, the driver avoided 4th Street.
   D. The driver avoided 4th Street being paved recently.

Lesson 2 continued:

Vocabulary: Choosing the Right Use

The following sentences contain vocabulary words used in the reading passage. Identify the sentence or sentences that use the italicized vocabulary word properly. We have changed the form of some vocabulary words to provide new contexts; for example, some adjectives and verbs have been used as nouns.

1) A. My dad's old cassette tapes are *obsolete*, but they still work.
   B. Some politicians harbor *obsolete* policies that do not agree with the new generation's beliefs.
   C. Dana was praised by critics for wearing an *obsolete* dress on the red carpet.
   D. Tim bought an *obsolete* computer so that he could use the newest programs.

2) A. Although some Great Whites do grow to be twenty-two feet in length, it is not *plausible* for them to become as large as the shark in the movie *Jaws*.
   B. Winning the lottery is a very *plausible* retirement plan.
   C. Randy failed to realize the *plausible* outcome of hitting the tetherball until it was too late.
   D. The team's *plausible* success is weighed entirely on the skill of the goalie.

3) A. The owners of the new bakery filed for *bankruptcy* once they found out they had cleared their first quarter.
   B. Despite the poor state of the economy, the CEO's smart spending habits kept her company safe from *bankruptcy*.
   C. The politician's moral *bankruptcy* allowed him to accept monetary bribes in exchange for favors.
   D. You do not need to ask for a loan if your business is nearing *bankruptcy*.

4) A. The door-to-door salesman insisted that there was a *resurgence* of typewriters as a part of his pitch to the buyer.
   B. Investors are hesitant to put any more of their money into the stock market until there is a *resurgence* of a strong market.
   C. The *resurgence* of earthquakes in California has allowed response teams to focus their attention on forest fires.
   D. On the eastern shore, erosion is obvious in the *resurgence* of soil and rock from the water onto the land.

5) A. The fishermen caught so much tuna that they could easily *accommodate* it all.
   B. The couple was looking for a new home that could *accommodate* the large family they hoped to have one day.
   C. The distracted barista over-poured the coffee so that the mug *accommodated* the liquid and spilled over the sides.
   D. Although the seams are stretched a little, the suit *accommodates* the large man well enough.

Lesson 2 continued:

6) A. The fortuneteller looked into her crystal ball and *augured* the customer's successful career.
   B. The dark clouds and fleeing birds *augured* the approaching storm.
   C. Insufficient evidence has led the scientists to *augur* with confidence.
   D. The author's intricate imagery *augured* the events of long-forgotten battles.

7) A. The massive asteroid tumbled slowly as it *gravitated* toward the planet at high speed.
   B. Thomas's rude manners and unhygienic tendencies *gravitated* Elsa to him.
   C. The pitcher's baseball *gravitated* toward the catcher's mitt.
   D. The *Harry Potter* fan *gravitated* toward the fantasy section of the library.

8) A. The *tactile* sound of the music brought the audience to their feet.
   B. Photos of the beach are nothing compared to the *tactile* feelings of warm sand and cool ocean water.
   C. The *tactile* feedback function of the phone causes it to vibrate when numbers on the screen are touched.
   D. Campfire smoke is a *tactile* gray that leaves its smell on your clothes for days.

9) A. People diagnosed with Alzheimer's disease are often advised to play memory games that improve their ability to *recollect* past events.
   B. Morrie would have received a better grade on his test if he had been able to *recollect* the answers he had studied the night before.
   C. The spectators could see the new contestant try to *recollect* the best way to go through the obstacle course.
   D. Nancy had obviously *recollected* the recipe, as the cake was falling apart and tasteless.

10) A. When a puppy behaves poorly, some may think the animal is *inherently* bad instead of realizing that it requires proper training.
    B. Breaking out of his routine, Jerry *inherently* decided to turn left instead of going right.
    C. While making pancakes, Franny added chocolate chips *inherently* even though she was on a diet.
    D. I am not sure if Ursula is *inherently* kind or if she just wants something from me.

Lesson 2 continued:

Synonyms and Antonyms

Match the word with its *antonym*.

1)	obsolete	**A.**	unbelievable
2)	plausible	**B.**	forget
3)	recollect	**C.**	unnaturally
4)	gravitate	**D.**	modern
5)	inherently	**E.**	retreat

Match the word with its *synonym*.

6)	bankruptcy	**A.**	revival
7)	augur	**B.**	contain
8)	resurgence	**C.**	failure
9)	tactile	**D.**	predict
10)	accommodate	**E.**	touchable

END of LESSON 2

Lesson 3

Questions 21–30 are based on the following passage.

This passage is adapted from Theodore Roosevelt's speech, "The Strenuous Life," to the Hamilton Club in 1899.

In speaking to you, men of the greatest city of the West, men of the State which gave to the country Lincoln and Grant, men who **preeminently** and distinctly embody all that is most American in the American character, I wish to preach, not the doctrine of **ignoble** ease, but the doctrine of the strenuous life, the life of toil and effort, of labor and strife; to preach that highest form of success which comes, not to the man who desires mere easy peace, but to the man who does not shrink from danger, from hardship, or from bitter toil, and who out of these wins the splendid ultimate triumph.

A life of **slothful** ease, a life of that peace which springs merely from lack either of desire or of power to strive after great things, is as little worthy of a nation as of an individual. I ask only that what every self-respecting American demands from himself and from his sons shall be demanded of the American nation as a whole. Who among you would teach your boys that ease, that peace, is to be the first consideration in their eyes—to be the ultimate goal after which they strive? You men of Chicago have made this city great, you men of Illinois have done your share, and more than your share, in making America great, because you neither preach nor practice such a doctrine. You work yourselves, and you bring up your sons to work. If you are rich and are worth your salt, you will teach your sons that though they may have leisure, it is not to be spent in **idleness**; for wisely used leisure merely means that those who possess it, being free from the necessity of working for their livelihood, are all the more bound to carry on some kind of non-**remunerative** work in science, in letters, in art, in exploration, in historical research—work of the type we most need in this country, the successful carrying out of which reflects most honor upon the nation. We do not admire the man of timid peace. We admire the man who embodies victorious effort; the man who never wrongs his neighbor, who is prompt to help a friend, but who has those **virile** qualities necessary to win in the **stern** strife of actual life. It is hard to fail, but it is worse never to have tried to succeed. In this life we get nothing save by effort. Freedom from effort in the present merely means that there has been stored up effort in the past. A man can be freed from the necessity of work only by the fact that he or his fathers before him have worked to good purpose. If the freedom thus purchased is used right, and the man still does actual work, though of a different kind, whether as a writer or a general, whether in the field of politics or in the field of exploration and adventure, he shows he deserves his good fortune. But if he treats this period of freedom from the need of actual labor as a period, not of preparation, but of mere enjoyment, even though perhaps not of vicious enjoyment, he shows that he is simply a **cumberer** of the earth's surface, and he surely unfits himself to hold his own with his fellows if the need to do so should again arise. A mere life of ease is not in the end a very satisfactory life, and, above all, it is a life which ultimately unfits those who follow it for serious work in the world.

As it is with the individual, so it is with the nation. It is a base untruth to say that happy is the nation that has no history. Thrice happy is the nation that has a glorious history. Far better it is to dare mighty things, to win glorious triumphs, even though checkered by failure, than to take rank with those poor spirits who neither enjoy much nor suffer much, because they live in the gray twilight that knows not victory nor defeat. If in 1861 the men who loved the Union had believed that peace was the end of all things, and war and strife the worst of all things, and had acted up to their belief, we would have saved hundreds of thousands of lives, we would have saved hundreds of millions of dollars. Moreover, besides saving all the blood and treasure we then **lavished**, we would have prevented the heartbreak of many women, the dissolution of many homes, and we would have spared the country those months of gloom and shame when it seemed as if our

Lesson 3 continued:

armies marched only to defeat. We could have avoided all this suffering simply by shrinking from strife. And if we had thus avoided it, we would have shown that we were weaklings, and that we were unfit to stand among the great nations of the earth. Thank God for the iron in the blood of our fathers, the men who upheld the wisdom of Lincoln, and bore sword or rifle in the armies of Grant! Let us, the children of the men who proved themselves equal to the mighty days, let us, the children of the men who carried the great Civil War to a triumphant conclusion, praise the God of our fathers that the ignoble **counsels** of peace were rejected; that the suffering and loss, the blackness of sorrow and despair, were unflinchingly faced, and the years of strife endured; for in the end the slave was freed, the Union restored, and the mighty American **republic** placed once more as a helmeted queen among nations.

21

Based on his commentary about the type of life one should live, which endeavor would the author reject as unacceptable?

A) to explore uncharted worlds without reward
B) to build a fortune and then live a life of comfort
C) to start a company at great financial risk, and ultimately fail
D) to labor in a factory for a lifetime to provide for one's family

22

In lines 25-35, the author claims that wealthy people are obligated to

A) ensure the sources of their wealth succeed.
B) distribute their wealth among the most poor.
C) employ people to make discoveries.
D) work toward advances in the arts and sciences.

23

As it is used in line 32, the term *non-remunerative* most nearly means

A) scientific.
B) unpaid.
C) part-time.
D) unimportant.

24

Choose the statement that best restates lines 42-46 ("Freedom from…purpose").

A) If you enjoy some type of freedom, it is only because you or your ancestors earned it.
B) Those who never lose have simply never attempted to do anything.
C) An uneventful life is a blessing because only fools seek out conflict.
D) All types of freedom, including freedom from work, is purchased at a high price.

Lesson 3 continued:

25

Choose the line from paragraph 3 (lines 61-95) that exemplifies the author's statement used in the previous question (lines 42-46: "Freedom from…purpose").

A) Lines 62-63 ("It is…history")
B) Lines 64-68 ("Far better…defeat")
C) Lines 79-80 ("We could…strife")
D) Lines 87-92 ("let us…endured")

26

To the author, peace is not synonymous with

A) happiness.
B) wealth.
C) victory.
D) leisure.

27

What does the author cite as an example to support his opinion that peace is not "the end of all things" (line 70)?

A) the futility of war
B) the value of hard work
C) the necessity of the Civil War
D) the need for science

28

Choose the statement that best paraphrases lines 57-60 ("A mere…world").

A) Living the easy life is honorable, but it makes it difficult to stay good at a job.
B) The easy life might be satisfying, but it is not real work.
C) A person living an easy life will neither be satisfied personally nor able to do real work.
D) Not all people can live comfortably without returning to work in some capacity.

29

Paragraphs 2 and 3 (lines 13-60, 61-95) both illustrate the author's idea of living a productive life, but they differ in that

A) the author makes an argument for a strong army in paragraph 3, while paragraph 2 doesn't mention the military.
B) paragraph 2 discusses individual behavior, while paragraph 3 describes the relevance of the author's philosophy on a national level.
C) paragraph 2 focuses on wealth, while paragraph 3 expresses the author's grievances with younger generations.
D) paragraph 2 is a guide to conduct for society, while paragraph 3 is a guide for the nation.

30

Select the line from the passage that best supports your answer to the previous question.

A) Lines 79-80 ("We could…strife")
B) Lines 42-43 ("Freedom from…past")
C) Lines 74-76 ("Moreover…heartbreak")
D) Line 61 ("As it…nation")

Lesson 3 continued:

Vocabulary: Context Answers

The following sentences contain vocabulary words used in the reading passage. Choose the answer that best completes the sentence. There may be more than one technically correct answer, but one will better exemplify the italicized vocabulary word than the others will.

1) In the medical world, the duty of a doctor is *preeminently* _____.
   A. to treat patients' problems
   B. to cure dangerous diseases
   C. to send patients to a hospital
   D. to collect insurance money
   E. to learn about new treatments

2) The soldier was _____ his commander due to his *ignoble* behavior on the last mission.
   A. promoted by
   B. commended by
   C. ignored by
   D. forgotten by
   E. reprimanded by

3) Gina's *slothful* behavior _____ the production of the group project.
   A. encouraged
   B. delayed
   C. cancelled
   D. started
   E. eased

4) _____ will eventually lead to *idleness* in the workplace.
   A. Holding long conference calls
   B. Scheduling too many meetings
   C. Taking extended breaks
   D. Going out for company lunches
   E. Calling out sick

5) "It would be *remunerative* for you to _____," said William as he looked at his client's dwindling bank accounts.
   A. invest in the struggling café
   B. purchase a new car
   C. store your money in a safe
   D. donate to your favorite charity
   E. sell your beach house

6) Every morning before work, the *virile* young professional _____.
   A. hits the snooze button at least five times
   B. runs three miles
   C. coughs for ten minutes
   D. gets dressed and eats breakfast
   E. complains about the noisy traffic

7) Henry's *stern* expression showed his _____ the puppy's energetic antics.
   A. amusement toward
   B. acceptance of
   C. hatred toward
   D. disapproval of
   E. knowledge of

8) Bad economic times proved to be a *cumberer* of the country's _____.
   A. downfall
   B. progress
   C. creation
   D. inactivity
   E. history

Lesson 3 continued:

9) The Olympic diving team was *lavished* _____ after the awards ceremony.
   A. with praise
   B. in the news
   C. with boos
   D. upon the stage
   E. with adoring fans

10) Owen offered heartfelt *counsel*s to the _____ young woman.
   A. unknown
   B. bored
   C. smart
   D. attractive
   E. troubled

11) Unlike a monarchy, the supreme power in a *republic* is held by _____.
   A. a dictator
   B. the wealthy
   C. the citizens
   D. an emperor
   E. men only

Lesson 3 continued:

Writing Practice

Some of the following sentences are fragments, comma splices, or run-ons. Choose the answer that best corrects the sentence while retaining the intended meaning of the original sentence. Select NO CHANGE if the provided sentence is correct.

1) Few fans attended the final game of the season the team had lost every game prior to it.
   A. NO CHANGE
   B. Few fans attended the final game of the season the team had lost every game prior to it was the reason.
   C. Few fans attended the final game of the season, the team had lost every game prior to it.
   D. Few fans attended the final game of the season because the team had lost every game prior to it.

2) The family's dinner was interrupted when the storm hit, and all the power in the house went out for hours.
   A. NO CHANGE
   B. The family's dinner, which was interrupted when the storm hit, and all the power in the house went out for hours.
   C. The family's dinner; it was interrupted when the storm hit and all the power in the house went out for hours.
   D. The family's dinner, interrupted when the storm hit, and all the power in the house went out for hours.

3) Last Friday night, my roommates and I decided that instead of going to the party.
   A. NO CHANGE
   B. We didn't go to the party last Friday we had too much homework to do.
   C. Instead of going to the party last Friday night, my roommates and I decided to watch a movie.
   D. My roommates and I decided not to go to the party last Friday night, we watched a movie instead.

4) Karen, her car abandoned on the side of the highway during the snowstorm.
   A. NO CHANGE
   B. Karen had to abandon her car on the side of the highway during the snowstorm.
   C. During the snowstorm the car on the side of the highway. Karen abandoned it.
   D. Karen's car on the side of the highway. It was during a snowstorm.

5) Biology was my favorite subject in college, it has allowed me to become a research scientist.
   A. NO CHANGE
   B. Biology, being my favorite subject in college, it has allowed me to become a research scientist.
   C. Biology was my favorite subject in college. It has allowed me to become a research scientist.
   D. My favorite subject in college was biology it has allowed me to become a research scientist.

Lesson 3 continued:

6) Cheating on the exam during calculus and Lula was caught by the teacher.
   A. NO CHANGE
   B. The teacher caught Lula cheating on the exam she thought it was difficult.
   C. Lula, cheating on her exam during calculus. She was caught by the teacher.
   D. The teacher caught Lula cheating on the calculus exam.

7) Whitewater rafting in Costa Rica last summer with my family while on vacation.
   A. NO CHANGE
   B. Whitewater rafting and vacation with my family was fun. Because we were in Costa Rica.
   C. While on vacation with my family last summer in Costa Rica, we went whitewater rafting.
   D. In Costa Rica last summer with my family. Whitewater rafting on the most intense river was difficult.

8) Pepperoni pizza from the Italian restaurant in town is my favorite the taste is authentic.
   A. NO CHANGE
   B. My favorite pepperoni pizza is from the Italian restaurant in town because the taste is authentic.
   C. The pizza is authentic from the Italian restaurant in town owned by Italians my favorite is pepperoni.
   D. The authentic pizza from the Italian restaurant is my favorite, it's the pepperoni.

9) When Jeanine goes to concerts and finds herself dancing around, singing to songs, and having a great time.
   A. NO CHANGE
   B. When Jeanine goes to concerts; she finds herself dancing around, singing to songs, and having a great time.
   C. When Jeanine goes to concerts, she finds herself dancing around, singing to songs, and having a great time.
   D. When Jeanine, who goes to concerts, and finds herself dancing around, singing to songs, and having a great time.

10) Renee's five-year-old son threw a tantrum at his birthday party he hated the ice cream cake she had bought for him.
   A. NO CHANGE
   B. Renee's five-year-old son, who threw a tantrum at his birthday party, because he hated the ice cream cake she had bought for him.
   C. Renee's five-year-old son threw a tantrum at his birthday party because he hated the ice cream cake she had bought for him.
   D. Renee's five-year-old son threw a tantrum at his birthday party he hated the ice cream cake, which she had bought for him.

Lesson 3 continued:

11) In a rush, Carl ran down the hill, jumped the creek, and raced up the porch steps he had to make it home before curfew.
   A. NO CHANGE
   B. In a rush, Carl ran down the hill, jumped the creek, and raced up the porch steps in order to make it home before curfew.
   C. Carl had to make it home before curfew, in a rush, he ran down the hill, jumped the creek, and raced up the porch.
   D. Carl, in a rush, ran down the hill, jumped the creek, and raced up the porch steps, he had to make it home before curfew.

12) Grace didn't realize that joining the choir and singing during the concert would strain her vocal cords, resulting in a raspy voice.
   A. NO CHANGE
   B. Grace didn't realize when joining the choir, and singing to accompany the concert, straining her vocal cords, would result in rasping.
   C. Grace didn't realize, joining and singing in the choir. The concert would strain her vocal cords, resulting in rasping.
   D. Grace didn't realize the concert would strain her vocal cords, result in a rasping voice so she joined the choir.

13) As the server was carrying the large steaming plates of spaghetti and ravioli through the crowded restaurant.
   A. NO CHANGE
   B. Meanwhile, the server was carrying the large steaming plates of spaghetti and ravioli through the crowded restaurant, he tripped.
   C. The server was carrying the large steaming plates of spaghetti and ravioli through the crowded restaurant.
   D. While the server carried the large steaming plates of spaghetti and ravioli through the crowded restaurant.

14) The weather at the beach was perfect, and the waves were ideal for surfing, so we decided to stay all day.
   A. NO CHANGE
   B. We decided to stay all day and surf, the weather at the beach was perfect, and the waves were ideal.
   C. The weather at the beach. The waves were ideal for surfing so we decided to stay all day.
   D. We decided to stay at the beach; the ideal waves and perfect weather.

15) The smartphone, which could be hooked up to either a tablet or a personal computer.
   A. NO CHANGE
   B. Allowing the smartphone to be hooked up to either a tablet or a personal computer.
   C. One type of smartphone, which could be hooked up to either a tablet or a personal computer.
   D. The smartphone, which could be hooked up to either a tablet or a personal computer, cost too much.

Lesson 3 continued:

Vocabulary: Choosing the Right Use

The following sentences contain vocabulary words used in the reading passage. Identify the sentence or sentences that use the italicized vocabulary word properly. We have changed the form of some vocabulary words to provide new contexts; for example, some adjectives and verbs have been used as nouns.

1) A. The wrestler flexed and grinned *preeminently* when his name was announced as he entered the ring.
   B. Susan's resume proves that she is *preeminently* qualified for the job.
   C. Lions are the *preeminent* carnivores in this part of the savannah.
   D. The children were not *preeminent* to check out Young Adult novels.

2) A. The soldier's *ignoble* conduct earned him a medal of honor.
   B. When Jerry decided to return the wallet to its owner, his parents said it was very *ignoble* of him.
   C. The senator's *ignoble* actions prevented him from being reelected.
   D. Terry thought it was *ignoble* of her boyfriend to refuse to hold the door open for her.

3) A. The *slothful* movements of the snail as it made its way across the lawn were boring to watch.
   B. My new computer runs so smooth and *slothful* that I gave it a great review.
   C. The cyclist set a *slothful* pace that allowed her to set a personal record.
   D. If Garrett does not improve his *slothful* work ethic, his project will never be finished on time.

4) A. Robin had been traveling for so long that his *idleness* was exhausting him.
   B. The old fisherman found peace in the *idleness* of sitting motionless and fishing for hours on end, even when his chances of catching anything were negligible.
   C. The car sat in *idleness* for so long that the paint had faded and the metal had rusted.
   D. Your *idleness* impressed your group members so much that they gave you an excellent grade.

5) A. Since Katie's dog went missing, she has been posting flyers advertising a *remunerative* reward for anyone who finds her pet.
   B. Ever since John lost his job, he has been living off *remunerative* welfare.
   C. If you want to live in New York City, you need a *remunerative* job in order to afford rent.
   D. After the drought of the season, the farmers were left with a *remunerative* crop.

Lesson 3 continued:

6) A. Jake was so concerned with maintaining his *virile* image that he bought only brand-name items.
   B. Because society dictates that facial hair is a *virile* trait, women are encouraged to tweeze their eyebrows and wax above their lips.
   C. Lions seem impressive and *virile*, but it is the lionesses who hunt for the pride.
   D. The portrait of the queen depicted her as regal, rich, and *virile*.

7) A. The principal's *stern* expression put the student's mind at ease when he was called into the office.
   B. Connor ignored his mother's requests to set the table until her voice took on a *stern* tone.
   C. The *stern* state of the boat suggested that it had not been damaged in the hurricane.
   D. The country's *stern* insistence on fair trials means that it takes its citizens' rights seriously.

8) A. The lifted weight of the rubble was a *cumberer* to the rescued victims of the cave-in.
   B. Girl Scouts volunteered to *cumber* the building of the playground.
   C. The athlete's old injury became a real *cumberer* to her success when arthritis began affecting the joint.
   D. George found himself a home-healthcare nurse when his health began to fail because he didn't want to be a *cumberer* to his family.

9) A. The patient's bedside table was *lavished* with flowers and get well cards.
   B. Brian was pleased that the gas station employees had refueled his car and *lavished* it with a car wash.
   C. The homeowners *lavished* their house with chandeliers and famous paintings.
   D. The path of the tornado left behind *lavished* piles of debris and rubble.

10) A. It is often said that the best *counsel* comes from the elderly and the experienced.
    B. The *counsels* of my parents and high school advisor helped me narrow down my college choices.
    C. The *counsels* of science do not yet allow time travel or the resurrection of animals long since extinct.
    D. Carter blamed the *counsels* of violent television shows for his destructive behavior.

11) A. The club's *republic* met every first Thursday of the month in order to discuss the upcoming events.
    B. Due to the recent decree made by the *republic*, all teenagers in the country are under curfew.
    C. After his father's passing, the prince was crowned king in a majestic ceremony held in the *republic*.
    D. The *republic* was divided by beliefs, and civil war soon broke out.

Lesson 3 continued:

Synonyms and Antonyms

Match the word with its *antonym*.

1) ignoble	**A.** lenient
2) slothful	**B.** weak
3) remunerative	**C.** industrious
4) virile	**D.** monarchy
5) stern	**E.** unprofitable
6) republic	**F.** honorable

Match the word with its *synonym*.

7) preeminently	**A.** obstructer
8) idleness	**B.** shower
9) cumberer	**C.** notably
10) lavish	**D.** advice
11) counsel	**E.** laziness

END of LESSON 3

Lesson 4

Questions 31–41 are based on the following passage.

This passage details a growing ecological concern that originates with the devices intended to improve lives.

Gadget technology is improving at record rates, and users—half, at least—are compelled to upgrade their smartphones, tablet computers, video game consoles, and other electronic luxuries to the latest versions as soon as they become available. All this upgrading creates a **dilemma**: How should we dispose of the old gadgets? Electronic waste, or e-waste, has become one of the most important, **albeit** little discussed, environmental concerns of the modern age. A bigger trash can is not a solution because e-waste contains several hazardous elements, including mercury, lead, and cadmium, all of which can cause serious **adverse** medical effects and pollute indefinitely; besides, why would we want to scrap all the good things in e-waste, like copper, palladium, silver, and gold?

Presently, in the United States, approximately sixty percent of e-waste is thrown in the trash. Not only is the non-biodegradable e-waste taking up landfill space, but the aforementioned hazardous materials are **leaching** into the soil and poisoning the groundwater. Existing e-waste makes up just two percent of landfill trash, but it accounts for seventy percent of hazardous landfill waste. If it is not put in a landfill, trashed e-waste is incinerated, releasing toxic fumes into the atmosphere. In order to reduce environmental damage, Americans need to alter how they dispose of e-waste. The rational solution to the problem is to expand e-waste recycling efforts. Forty percent of e-waste is recycled currently, and some states have already banned the trash disposal of at least certain types of e-waste. Disposal laws, partnered with awareness efforts, could increase e-waste recycling participation. Unfortunately, the problem is not so easily solved.

Electronics are not designed to be recycled, so it is expensive to do so properly and safely; the cost often exceeds the value of the recoverable materials. Electronic recycling plants that are part of the e-Steward network process e-waste safely; however, industry experts estimate that fifty to eighty percent of e-waste collected by recyclers is sold to brokers who export it to developing countries such as China, India, and Ghana. Some of the devices in the shipments are usable or reparable, but the local markets are already **saturated** with used electronics. Scrappers, often teenagers working for extremely low wages, use hammers and pliers to tear apart the devices, **salvage** any precious metals for resale, and then take advantage of lenient disposal laws to **discard**, cheaply, the useless, but still hazardous, waste. For extremely low wages, workers, often children or teenagers, use **deleterious** methods to dismantle electronics. They smash cathode ray tubes, releasing harmful phosphorus dust into the atmosphere; they cook circuit boards over open flames to melt the lead solder while breathing the toxic lead fumes; they burn plastic housings and wire **sheaths**, sending plumes of acrid, black smoke into the sky. Laborers also dump pure acids and dissolved heavy metals into nearby water sources, unwittingly creating some of the most polluted bodies of water in the world.

Obviously, real recycling programs should not simply export the hazards to developing countries. The international community has acknowledged the issue. In 1989, cooperating nations endorsed the Basel Convention treaty to reduce the movement of hazardous waste between countries, specifically the transfer of toxic waste from developed to less developed countries. The 1995 Basel Ban amendment expanded the treaty to include recycling. Many nations around the world, including the entire European Union, have **ratified** the Basel Convention and its amendment; however, as of 2015, the United States is one of two countries (the second being Haiti) to sign but not ratify the Basel Convention. Pressuring the US to ratify the Basel Convention would help reduce toxic materials being shipped to developing countries, but it would not eliminate the problem, especially since the toxic trade benefits developing countries financially. Every dollar spent on e-waste recycling, legitimate or not, helps to grow the domestic electronic market of less developed countries and, in turn, the middle class.

The only **definitive** way to reduce e-waste is by rethinking electronics production from the start. Most electronics are not designed to be recycled, and almost all electronics are guaranteed to become outdated, if not obsolete, within short timeframes. Broken technology is almost always cheaper to replace than repair. Designing electronics that could be easily fixed or even upgraded without a full replacement would significantly reduce e-waste. With enough global pressure—customer demand, that is—tech companies will invent environmentally friendlier devices. For the time being, when the newest gadget comes out a few months after you bought your last one, take a moment to consider where your old device will end up.

Lesson 4 continued:

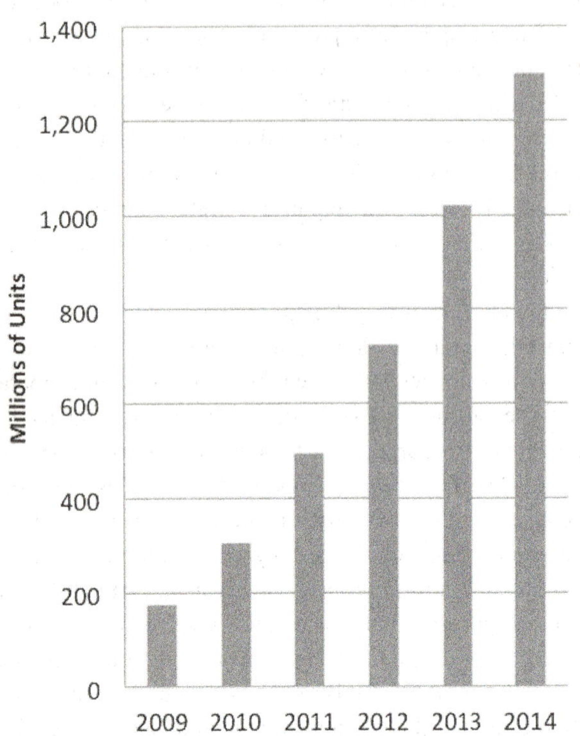

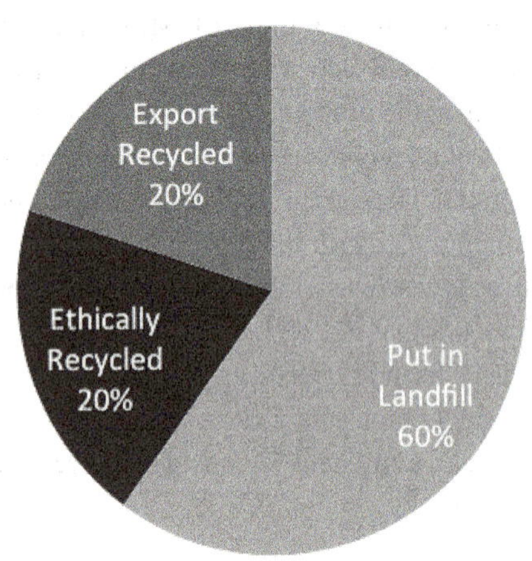

31

Choose the answer that best describes the purpose of paragraph 2 (lines 15-31).

A) the solution to e-waste disposal
B) present handling of e-waste
C) obstacles to the cleanup of toxic compounds
D) the future of e-waste disposal

32

In line 56, the author contrasts "real recycling programs" with the exportation of e-waste. From this statement, the reader can infer that

A) the author favors the export of e-waste because it simplifies its disposal.
B) e-waste contains too many valuable materials to be considered for recycling.
C) exporting e-waste is not actual recycling.
D) the process is the same, no matter what it is called.

33

If the author of the passage wanted to add an introductory sentence to paragraph 1 (lines 1-14), which one would be best?

A) Electronics might be small, but they create a large amount of waste.
B) Smartphones and small computers are constantly being upgraded and discarded.
C) Without electronics, life would change for the better.
D) Electronic treasures quickly turn into trash.

34

Which one of the following elements is described as being hazardous?

A) silver
B) palladium
C) cadmium
D) copper

Lesson 4 continued:

35

According to the passage, the central motive for recyclers' wanting to export e-waste to less developed countries is

A) ethical.
B) legal.
C) economic.
D) environmental.

36

Choose the line from the passage that provides the best evidence for your answer to the previous question.

A) Lines 5-8 ("All this…modern age")
B) Lines 32-39 ("Electronics…Ghana")
C) Lines 19-24 ("Existing…e-waste")
D) Lines 47-55 ("They smash…world")

37

Based on the data on the "Smartphones Sold Globally" chart, how did smartphone use change between 2010 and 2012?

A) more than doubled
B) decreased by half
C) increased by 1 billion
D) stayed nearly the same

38

As it is used in line 46, *deleterious* most nearly means

A) unplanned.
B) profitable.
C) unsafe.
D) indifferent.

39

Of the following elements of the e-waste disposal industry, which one is not acknowledged in the passage?

A) child labor
B) drug abuse
C) dangerous work
D) pollution

40

The subject of the last paragraph (lines 75-87) is best described as

A) differences in perspective.
B) scientific data on e-waste.
C) the problem at hand.
D) the real solution to e-waste.

41

What can be inferred from the wording chosen on the "Electronic Waste Disposal" chart?

A) More e-waste is recycled than put into landfills.
B) Exporting e-waste is unethical.
C) More e-waste is exported than recycled.
D) The number of landfills is growing rapidly.

Lesson 4 continued:

Vocabulary: Context Answers

The following sentences contain vocabulary words used in the reading passage. Choose the answer that best completes the sentence. There may be more than one technically correct answer, but one will better exemplify the italicized vocabulary word than the others will.

1) Quentin's moral *dilemma* convinced him to ask his father for _____.
   A. permission
   B. forgiveness
   C. an apology
   D. some advice
   E. the truth

2) Jonathan clearly, *albeit* _____, presented his speech to the class.
   A. quietly
   B. plainly
   C. sharply
   D. bravely
   E. distinctly

3) The *adverse* weather _____ the farmer's cornfield.
   A. nourished
   B. revived
   C. deprived
   D. intimidated
   E. destroyed

4) In order to prevent the vitamins from *leaching*, _____.
   A. Bill took three of them every morning
   B. the veterinarian prescribed a double-strength variety
   C. they were tightly sealed
   D. Margaret paid for them in advance
   E. companies sold them at a discount

5) The local art community was *saturated* _____ when the new studio opened in town.
   A. to its limit
   B. and needed more painters
   C. before the annual gallery show
   D. with new artists
   E. throughout the county

6) After the massive hurricane, we did not expect to *salvage* _____.
   A. through all the evacuation traffic
   B. a meeting with the police
   C. any of our belongings
   D. a little insurance money
   E. the flooded roadways

7) You should *discard* any _____ if you want to enjoy this twelve-mile hike.
   A. heavy, unnecessary items
   B. feelings of hope
   C. organic materials
   D. hiking boots
   E. maps of the summit

8) _____ is sure to have a *deleterious* effect on the neighborhood.
   A. Opening a new grocery store
   B. The low cost of living
   C. The high crime rate
   D. Building too many houses
   E. Closing the community pool

Lesson 4 continued:

9) The *sheaths* _____ the electric cables tore from the force of the lightning strike.
   A. fastening
   B. holding down
   C. exposing
   D. suspending
   E. covering

10) Without _____, we cannot *ratify* the new camp rules.
   A. looking at the cabins
   B. everyone's vote
   C. permission from the campers' parents
   D. the camp director's knowledge
   E. understanding how to run a summer camp

11) Despite years of research, the scientist could not find a *definitive* _____ to his hypothesis.
   A. reason
   B. problem
   C. solution
   D. cause
   E. meaning

Lesson 4 continued:

Writing Practice

The underlined portion of each sentence provides two pronouns that are often used incorrectly. Choose the pronoun that completes the sentence correctly.

1) The panel was finally assembled, but <u>who</u> / <u>whom</u> arrived late?

2) The amateur cave explorer, <u>who</u> / <u>whom</u> the salesman had tricked into spending thousands of dollars, was carrying too much equipment.

3) This paperwork for the New York City trip should be filled out by <u>who</u> / <u>whom</u>?

4) Why do those two have to guess <u>who</u> / <u>whom</u> started the fight instead of finishing it?

5) In the people <u>who</u> / <u>whom</u> lived above the clouds, there lurked a fear of the mists below.

6) Prowling in the barn at night was Bill, <u>who</u> / <u>whom</u> I nearly hit with a shovel.

7) The Academy Award-winning director said, "To those <u>who</u> / <u>whom</u> helped me make it this far, I want to offer my sincerest gratitude."

8) Sondra and her sister went to the midnight movie with <u>who</u> / <u>whom</u>?

9) <u>Who</u> / <u>Whom</u> did they say was in charge of decorating for the Halloween party?

10) Evan, someone <u>who</u> / <u>whom</u> his brother had once idolized, turned out to be a terrible role model.

11) Justin, <u>who</u> / <u>whom</u> is a photography fan, received a new camera for Christmas.

12) <u>Who</u> / <u>Whom</u> could Molly trust to help her with the homework that she needed to complete by tomorrow?

13) Gail, <u>who</u> / <u>whom</u> is a talented musician, as well as a composer, won first chair at the state symphony festival.

14) My mother asked <u>who</u> / <u>whom</u> could host the Jeopardy show after Alex Trebek retires.

15) Isaac's mother worried about her son and asked her eldest daughter, "After his car broke down, Isaac got a ride from <u>who</u> / <u>whom</u>?"

Lesson 4 continued:

Vocabulary: Choosing the Right Use

The following sentences contain vocabulary words used in the reading passage. Identify the sentence or sentences that use the italicized vocabulary word properly. We have changed the form of some vocabulary words to provide new contexts; for example, some adjectives and verbs have been used as nouns.

1) A. Many students are faced with the *dilemma* of choosing between playing a sport or participating in club activities.
   B. The volunteers built bookcases for the new library, and their hard work created a *dilemma* for the librarians.
   C. In times of hardship, farmers may have the *dilemma* of choosing whether to feed their livestock or themselves.
   D. George's dessert was so good that it created a *dilemma* amongst the guests.

2) A. Larry looked great in his new suit, *albeit* very stylish, and Trish told him so when he walked into the office.
   B. I thought the horror movie was great, *albeit* the screams of the actors could have been more realistic.
   C. The captain of the ship was terrified of the legion of pirates he saw before him, *albeit* he did not want his crew to see his fear.
   D. Jackie's overweight, *albeit* hyperactive, Chihuahua greeted me when I came through the front door.

3) A. Harry's blood pressure medication might have prevented another heart attack, but the drug had *adverse* effects on his liver and kidneys.
   B. Food and water shortages created *adverse* conditions for the refugees during the first year of the war.
   C. We tried to get into the party, but the bouncer standing outside was an *adverse* to our entrance.
   D. The mariachi band's performance is *adverse* to Tony's usual music preference.

4) A. The elementary school children stared wide-eyed as the octopus's tentacles stretched out, *leaching* onto the glass of its tank.
   B. The landfill is lined with heavy plastic to prevent water passing through the trash from *leaching* into the ground.
   C. Walter's father scolded him because the soda Walter had spilled was *leaching* into the sofa cushions.
   D. The janitor grimaced when the gum lazy students left under the table *leached* to his hands.

5) A. Brittany's umbrella had broken, so she arrived home with her clothes *saturated* with water.
   B. I never get popcorn at the movies because it is always *saturated* with butter and salt.
   C. Meghan struggled to open the packaging around the chocolate bar as it was *saturated* in a foil covering.
   D. After the storm, the whole town was *saturated* in three feet of snow.

Lesson 4 continued:

6) A. Once they saw the wreckage on sonar, they were able to *salvage* valuables from the ship.
   B. A group had crowded around the teenager at the carnival game who hoped to *salvage* the teddy bear for his girlfriend.
   C. The archaeologists were prepared to *salvage* any artifacts they found during the excavation.
   D. The sharks circled the dead whale, hoping to *salvage* a meal from the carcass.

7) A. The shoplifters *discarded* the high-end designer clothes.
   B. Carrie dug through the refrigerator and *discarded* any food that had passed its expiration date.
   C. The first person to *discard* all of his or her cards in the game Uno wins.
   D. The skydivers double-checked their gear before they were *discarded* from the plane.

8) A. Underground atomic detonations have *deleterious* effects on the environment that persist long after the initial blast.
   B. As part of Zack's job as a computer specialist, he is supposed to set up defenses against any *deleterious* viruses.
   C. After the procedure, the doctors were praised for their *deleterious* techniques.
   D. The antique shop holds everything from vintage furniture to *deleterious* books.

9) A. Every pair of glasses comes with a cleaning kit and in a leather *sheath* to tighten the frame.
   B. The baker piped cream filling into doughy *sheaths* while hungry children peered through the shop window.
   C. Knights kept their swords in *sheaths* when not in battle so as to not accidentally cut themselves.
   D. When Sarah picked up her dry cleaning, her clothes were handed to her on hangers and wrapped in plastic *sheaths*.

10) A. The school bus driver *ratified* the students' pleas to listen to rap music on their way to the museum.
   B. Mayor Harris *ratified* the new laws to impose harsher restrictions on new drivers.
   C. Jewelers must *ratify* the quality of their gems before putting them on display.
   D. The artist's mentors *ratified* his work so that he could host an exhibition at the school.

11) A. Once a person contracts a virus, there is no *definitive* way to rid it from his or her body completely.
   B. My nail polish had been painted on my toes so *definitively* that I was upset when they were smudged.
   C. After years of random skirmishes and firefights after the agreed ceasefire, the leaders of both countries sought a *definitive* end to the war.
   D. Our teacher asked us to list the *definitive* types of rocks found near volcanoes.

Lesson 4 continued:

Synonyms and Antonyms

Match the word with its *antonym*.

1) dilemma	**A.** dry
2) adverse	**B.** retain
3) saturated	**C.** supportive
4) salvage	**D.** imprecise
5) discard	**E.** solution
6) definitive	**F.** abandon

Match the word with its *synonym*.

7) albeit	**A.** soak
8) leach	**B.** covering
9) deleterious	**C.** although
10) sheath	**D.** approve
11) ratify	**E.** dangerous

END of LESSON 4

Lesson 5

Questions 42–52 are based on the following passages.

Passage 1 is adapted from John Dickinson's speech to Congress in 1776. Passage 2 is adapted from Samuel Adams's speech at the State House, Philadelphia, in 1776.

Passage 1

It too often happens, fellow citizens, that men, heated by the spirit of party, give more importance in their discourses, to the surface and appearance of objects, than either to reason or justice; thus **evincing** that their aim is not to appease **tumults**, but to excite them; not to **repress** the passions, but to inflame them, not to compose ferocious **discords**, but to **exasperate** and embitter them more and more. They **aspire** but to please the powerful, to gratify their own ambition, to flatter the caprices of the multitude, in order to captivate their favor. Accordingly in popular commotions, the party of wisdom and of **equity** is commonly found in the minority; and, perhaps, it would be safer, in difficult circumstances, to consult the smaller instead of the greater number. Upon this principle I invite the attention of those who hear me, since my opinion may differ from that of the majority; but I dare believe it will be shared by all impartial and moderate citizens, who condemn this tumultuous proceeding, this attempt to **coerce** our opinions, and to drag us, with so much precipitation to the most serious and important of decisions. But, coming to the subject in controversy, I affirm that **prudent** men do not abandon objects which are certain, to go in pursuit of those which offer only uncertainty. Now, it is an established fact, that America can be well and happily governed by the English laws, under the same king and the same parliament. Two hundred years of happiness furnish the proof of it; and we find it also in the present prosperity, which is the result of these **venerable** laws and of this ancient union. It is not as independent, but as subjects; not as republic, but as monarchy, that we have arrived at this degree of power and of greatness.

. . . .

I know the name of liberty is dear to each one of us; but have we not enjoyed liberty even under the English monarchy? Shall we this day renounce that to go and seek it in I know not what form of republic, which will soon change into a **licentious** anarchy and popular tyranny? In the human body the head only sustains and governs all the members, directing them, with admirable harmony, to the same object, which is self-preservation and happiness; so the head of the body politic, that is the king, in concert with the parliament, can alone maintain the union of the members of this empire, lately so flourishing, and prevent civil war by obviating all the evils produced by variety of opinions and diversity of interests. And so firm is my persuasion of this, that I fully believe the most cruel war which Great Britain could make upon us, would be that of not making any; and that the surest means of bringing us back to her obedience, would be that of employing none. For the dread of the English arms once removed, provinces would rise up against provinces, and cities against cities; and we should be seen to turn against ourselves the arms we have taken up to combat the common enemy.

Insurmountable necessity would then **compel** us to resort to the **tutelary** authority which we should have rashly **abjured**, and if it consented to receive us again under its **aegis**, it would be no longer as free citizens, but as slaves.

Still inexperienced, and in our infancy, what proof have we given of our ability to walk without a guide? None, and, if we judge the future by the past, we must conclude that our **concord** will continue as long as the danger, and no longer.

Lesson 5 continued:

Passage 2

OUR forefathers, 'tis said, **consented** to be subject to the laws of Great Britain. I will not at the present time dispute it, nor mark out the limits and conditions of their submission; but will it be denied that they **contracted** to pay obedience and to be under the control of Great Britain because it appeared to them most beneficial in their then present circumstances and situations? We, my countrymen, have the same right to consult and provide for our happiness which they had to promote theirs. If they had a view to **posterity** in their contracts, it must have been to advance the **felicity** of their descendants. If they erred in their expectations and prospects, we can never be condemned for a conduct which they would have recommended had they foreseen our present condition.

Ye darkeners of counsel, who would make the property, lives, and religion of millions depend on the evasive interpretations of musty parchments; who would send us to **antiquated** charters of uncertain and contradictory meaning, to prove that the present generation are not bound to be victims to cruel and unforgiving **despotism**,—tell us whether our **pious** and generous ancestors bequeathed to us the miserable privilege of having the rewards of our honesty, industry, the fruits of those fields which they purchased and bled for, wrested from us at the will of men over whom we have no check. Did they contract for us that, with folded arms, we should expect that justice and mercy from brutal and inflamed invaders which have been denied to our **supplications** at the foot of the throne? Were we to hear our character as a people ridiculed with indifference? Did they promise for us that our meekness and patience should be insulted, our coasts harassed, our towns demolished and plundered, and our wives and offspring exposed to nakedness, hunger, and death, without our feeling the resentment of men, and exerting those powers of self-preservation which God has given us?

....

Men who content themselves with the semblance of truth, and a display of words talk much of our obligations to Great Britain for protection. Had she a single eye to our advantage? A nation of shopkeepers are very seldom so interested. Let us not be so amused with words! The extension of her commerce was her object. When she defended our coasts, she fought for her customers, and convoyed our ships loaded with wealth, which we had acquired for her by our industry. She has treated us as beasts of burden, whom the lordly masters cherish that they may carry a greater load. Let us inquire also against whom she has protected us? Against her own enemies with whom we had no quarrel, or only on her account, and against whom we always readily exerted our wealth and strength when they were required. Were these Colonies backward in giving assistance to Great Britain, when they were called upon in 1739 to aid the expedition against Cartagena? They at that time sent three thousand men to join the British army, although the war commenced without their consent.

....

Who among you, my countrymen, that is a father, would claim authority to make your child a slave because you had nourished him in infancy?

'Tis a strange species of generosity which requires a return infinitely more valuable than anything it could have bestowed; that demands as a reward for a defense of our property a surrender of those inestimable privileges to the **arbitrary** will of **vindictive tyrants**, which alone give value to that very property.

Courage, then, my countrymen; our contest is not only whether we ourselves shall be free, but whether there shall be left to mankind an asylum on earth for civil and religious liberty. Dismissing, therefore, the justice of our cause as incontestable, the only question is, What is best for us to pursue in our present circumstances?

Lesson 5 continued:

42

The authors of both passages agree that British rule over the American colonies was

A) tolerable, except for the increasing taxes.
B) a threat to American stability.
C) sustainable through peace and diplomacy.
D) acceptable at least one time in history.

43

The answer to the previous question is something the authors agree on; now, choose the answer that best describes how the authors disagree on the same issue.

A) Dickinson believes America still benefits from English rule; Adams does not.
B) Adams believes that British rule is better for the economy.
C) Dickinson supports independence through war, while Adams demands diplomacy.
D) Adams doubts the good intentions of his ancestors, while Dickinson does not.

44

From Passage 2, lines 16-27 ("Ye darkeners…check"), a reader can infer that

A) Adams believes that the first American colonists lived decadently, without thought of future generations.
B) the author believes that previous agreements with Great Britain are outdated and detrimental to his generation.
C) the English laws were fair and impartial and the best hope for maintaining stability in America.
D) Adams's sentiment represents that of the majority of Americans of his time.

45

Identify the words used from the context of lines 16-27 ("Ye darkeners…check") that best support your answer to the previous question.

A) bound; charters
B) darkeners; religion
C) privilege; check
D) musty; antiquated

46

As it is used in Passage 2, line 30, *supplications* most nearly means

A) privileges.
B) demands.
C) pleas.
D) rations.

47

In Passage 1, Dickinson predicts that severing ties with Great Britain will result in

A) chaos and oppression.
B) no significant change for the better or worse.
C) productivity but less stability.
D) alliances with France and Spain.

Lesson 5 continued:

48

Choose the line from Passage 1 that provides the best evidence to support your answer to the previous question.

A) Lines 21-24 ("But…uncertainty")
B) Lines 34-36 ("I know…monarchy")
C) Lines 36-39 ("Shall we…tyranny")
D) Lines 47-49 ("And so…making any")

49

As it is used in Passage 1, line 19, *coerce* most nearly means

A) convince.
B) pressure.
C) motivate.
D) ask.

50

The "danger" Dickinson mentions in Passage 1, line 65, refers to

A) an unstable government.
B) the risk of economic collapse.
C) a civil war.
D) a war with Great Britain.

51

What, according to the author of Passage 1, is the cost of independence?

A) America would create its own form of monarchy.
B) The new ruler of America would engage in perpetual wars.
C) America would return to British rule and lose the freedom it had.
D) Great Britain would abandon its economic interests in America, rendering it barren and poor.

52

Choose the line from Passage 1 that provides the best evidence for your answer to the previous question.

A) Lines 56-60 ("Insurmountable…slaves")
B) Lines 43-47 ("the king…interests")
C) Lines 39-42 ("In the human…happiness")
D) Lines 63-65 ("None…longer")

Lesson 5 continued:

Vocabulary: Context Answers

The following sentences contain vocabulary words used in the reading passages. Choose the answer that best completes the sentence. There may be more than one technically correct answer, but one will better exemplify the italicized vocabulary word than the others will.

1) The crowd erupted in screams at the arrival of the actor, *evincing* _____.
   A. him to retreat into the theater
   B. their admiration toward him
   C. the security guards to form a barrier
   D. a smile to form on his face
   E. the man's nervousness

2) _____ sent the beachgoers into a *tumult.*
   A. A single cloud in the sky
   B. The lifeguard's departure
   C. A passing group of fishing boats
   D. The sighting of a shark
   E. A flock of noisy seagulls

3) As she heard the loud music in the club, Marie found it difficult to *repress* her _____.
   A. indifference
   B. silence
   C. excitement
   D. apathy
   E. phone call

4) Because there was *discord* among the members, the committee _____.
   A. decided to break for lunch
   B. found an answer to that day's problem
   C. voted to elect new members
   D. asked the chairman to speak
   E. was unable to agree on a solution

5) _____ is sure to *exasperate* the babysitter.
   A. Letting the toddler take a nap
   B. The little boy's stubbornness
   C. Taking a trip to the neighborhood playground
   D. The child's happy laughter
   E. Watching a movie

6) Because he *aspired* to become a novelist, Steve _____.
   A. paid close attention to the structure of classic novels
   B. saved his money until he had enough to hire a ghostwriter
   C. received a scholarship to play on the tennis team
   D. kept his writing secret
   E. bought every magazine he could afford

Lesson 5 continued:

7) Mr. Edwards, a respectable judge, believes _____ *equity*.
   A. criminals do not deserve
   B. lawyers should not receive
   C. both lawyers and criminals should not trust
   D. the jury can make a decision without using
   E. in treating each court case with

8) _____ *coerced* Vera into selling her family's farm.
   A. A huge amount of money
   B. Her lack of interest finally
   C. Living twenty miles away
   D. Moving to the city
   E. Liam's threats eventually

9) It would be *prudent* for Clarice to _____ while she attends college.
   A. join several different student organizations
   B. go to parties on the weekends
   C. spend her money wisely
   D. sign up for too many classes
   E. keep in touch with her high school friends

10) The *venerable* general's troops _____ his orders.
   A. spoke out against
   B. respectfully followed
   C. hesitantly followed
   D. decided to ignore
   E. disobeyed

11) Theresa's *licentious* behavior will soon _____ unless she starts acting differently.
   A. lead to a promotion
   B. reveal her true personality
   C. get her into trouble
   D. influence her friend's decisions
   E. put an end to her troubles

12) Though we were faced with almost *insurmountable* obstacles, we _____ the other football team.
   A. played
   B. defeated
   C. opposed
   D. stunned
   E. lost to

13) Confronted _____, we were *compelled* to answer the older man's questions.
   A. with a firm handshake
   B. with threats of violence
   C. against the wall
   D. with many problems
   E. in front of a bank

14) The native islanders formed a *tutelary* relationship with the explorers, promising to _____.
   A. ignore their pleas for help
   B. submit to their customs
   C. respect their elders
   D. teach them how to survive
   E. obey them in business matters

Lesson 5 continued:

15) Under the *aegis* of her experienced boss, Leann _____ as an employee.
    A. flopped
    B. blundered
    C. failed
    D. started
    E. prospered

16) The two parties worked in *concord*, reaching an agreement _____.
    A. through long arguments
    B. hesitantly
    C. that satisfied both of them
    D. despite running out of time
    E. to meet at a later date

17) Because _____, Mrs. Anderson *consented* to move forward with the plan.
    A. only one person thought it was wise
    B. she agreed with the strategy
    C. she assumed it would be a failure
    D. arguing is her passion
    E. there was time for debate

18) The two small countries *contracted* _____ in order to defend themselves from the invaders.
    A. to form an alliance
    B. to fight each other
    C. peaceful protests
    D. to leave each other alone
    E. a new law

19) The archivist _____ all the president's speeches for *posterity*.
    A. underlined the errors in
    B. sold copies of
    C. deleted the files of
    D. thoroughly studied
    E. kept a record of

20) As I _____, I felt an overwhelming sense of *felicity*.
    A. held my high school diploma
    B. received news of my cousin's car accident
    C. passed the basketball to Jose
    D. watched the frog jump into the calm pond
    E. listened to the conversations around me

21) _____, Jennifer looked thoughtfully at the *antiquated* map of the coastline.
    A. Sitting in her sports car
    B. On the fishing dock
    C. Aboard her friend's newest sailboat
    D. At the naval museum
    E. Standing next to the boardwalk's entrance

22) Because she grew up in a *pious* family, Laura was in the habit of _____.
    A. expressing her opinions
    B. using good manners
    C. getting along with strangers
    D. praying every day
    E. keeping to herself

Lesson 5 continued:

23) The *arbitrary* leader of the group _____.
   A. was quick to abandon his followers
   B. had been chosen at random
   C. earned no one's trust
   D. respected her followers' opinions
   E. had no control over anyone

24) Marcus and Elaine, the two head managers, were nothing but *tyrants* who _____.
   A. paid attention to detail
   B. followed the rules
   C. did not want their employees to argue
   D. abused their power
   E. questioned their bosses

Lesson 5 continued:

Writing Practice

The underlined portion of each sentence possibly contains a flaw related to the construction of the sentence. Select the answer that best corrects the flaw. Select NO CHANGE if the underlined portion is correct.

1) "The sidewalks are icy, so make sure you walk slowly, carefully, and to be safe," advised Grandma.
   A. NO CHANGE
   B. in a safe manner
   C. safely
   D. being safe

2) The brochure outlines many of the resort's details: complimentary Internet access, someone helping you find nearby restaurants, and private beach area.
   A. NO CHANGE
   B. nearby
   C. where there are nearby
   D. how to find nearby

3) After he disabled the alarm and stealing jewels from the museum, the felon escaped to Mexico under a fake name.
   A. NO CHANGE
   B. a disabling of the alarm
   C. the alarm was disabled
   D. disabling the alarm

4) Frederick spent about an hour searching for his notebook; he was trying to look in his bedroom and even checked the kitchen.
   A. NO CHANGE
   B. would try to look
   C. looked
   D. will try looking

5) The population of China is much larger than that of the United States, according to my geography professor.
   A. NO CHANGE
   B. than the United States
   C. than in the United States
   D. than the United States is

Lesson 5 continued:

6) <u>Soldiers from Germany</u>, Italian soldiers, and Japanese soldiers, who made up the Axis Powers, fought in World War II.
   A. NO CHANGE
   B. The Germans
   C. Germany
   D. German soldiers

7) "I love the zoo, and <u>animals are loved by me</u>, but I do not love this smell," Leroy explained, as we wandered around the monkey exhibit.
   A. NO CHANGE
   B. I love animals
   C. loving animals
   D. the animals

8) The <u>first</u>, second, and third person in line for concert tickets received a free band T-shirt.
   A. NO CHANGE
   B. first person
   C. first person in line
   D. person who was first

9) Vivian hoped <u>she would travel</u> to many foreign countries, to write about her observations, and to be discovered by a book publisher after she graduated from college.
   A. NO CHANGE
   B. traveling
   C. to travel
   D. travel would happen

10) Viewing the sparkling lights reflected in the lake water that evening made Michele feel <u>sadness</u>, but hopeful and thoughtful, too.
   A. NO CHANGE
   B. sadly
   C. with sadness
   D. sad

Lesson 5 continued:

Vocabulary: Choosing the Right Use

The following sentences contain vocabulary words used in the reading passages. Identify the sentence or sentences that use the italicized vocabulary word properly. We have changed the form of some vocabulary words to provide new contexts; for example, some adjectives and verbs have been used as nouns.

1) A. Myron spent many years trying to *repress* his memories of the bloody battle that only he and three other soldiers in his squad survived.
   B. The tyrant hoped that executing the outspoken dissidents would serve to *repress* any other thoughts of rebellion.
   C. Place a flower in between the pages of a book to *repress* its petals.
   D. Frank had to use a toothpick to dislodge the popcorn kernel that had *repressed* itself between his molars.

2) A. Constant *discord* between the two countries led to a war.
   B. Frustrated, Austen left the tangle of Christmas lights in a mess of *discords* on the floor by the tree.
   C. *Discord* among the players ensured that the team never made it to the semifinals.
   D. Miranda's growing nerves about the spelling bee engendered a *discord* in her.

3) A. After the marathon, the runners were breathless and *exasperated.*
   B. I do not wish to *exasperate* you, but could we take one more photo by the lake?
   C. As if to *exasperate* him, the server filled Sean's coffee mug so high that Sean could not avoid spilling it onto his hand.
   D. At the sound of thunder, the dog *exasperated* under a table.

4) A. Even though I did not go to college, I still *aspire* to become a famous architect.
   B. Judy's dream is to *aspire* wisdom and knowledge onto the students in her biology class.
   C. George always works hard because he *aspires* to take over the family business one day.
   D. The zombie lay in wait on the haunted trail and hoped he would *aspire* fear into the unsuspecting trick-or-treaters.

5) A. While I *coerce* the flour into the mixture, can you measure out two cups of sugar?
   B. After hours of trying to *coerce* a confession out of the suspect, the officers played "good cop, bad cop" with minimal success.
   C. With all eyes on the hypnotist, the audience was *coerced* into a deep sleep.
   D. The crime boss tried to *coerce* witnesses to the murder by threatening to harm them if they spoke to police.

Lesson 5 continued:

6) A. Before she left for her business trip, Janie was *prudent* enough to leave her appliances plugged in and the front door unlocked.
   B. You can tell me that the back seat of my car is a mess, but you do not have to be so *prudent* about it.
   C. The *prudent* commander risked the lives of his soldiers only when there was no alternative way to complete the mission.
   D. When Frank decided to move out, his *prudent* father suggested that he organize his belongings into the boxes based on the room where they should go.

7) A. The *venerable* elder was held in high regard for his knowledge about the land and the history of his people.
   B. The returning three-time champion was as *venerable* to her competitors as she was intimidating.
   C. In most cases, to act in self-defense is *venerable* and understandable in the eyes of the law.
   D. Todd's cab driver was *venerable* by taking him to his destination in the quickest time possible.

8) A. Ernie and his baseball team were late to the game because their bus had been stuck in a seemingly *insurmountable* traffic jam.
   B. Many thought that the conditions atop Mount Everest were *insurmountable* until the first successful ascent in 1953.
   C. Critics were shocked when the B-rated film had an *insurmountable* number of moviegoers attend the midnight premiere.
   D. The rock star won numerous awards for her *insurmountable* albums, especially the first two.

9) A. The bared teeth and growl of the dog *compelled* the burglar to climb slowly back out the window of the home he had broken into.
   B. The letter Jonah received in the mail today *compels* him about his aunt's poor health.
   C. The grotesque poster portraying photos of skin cancer *compelled* Audrey, who burns easily, to buy a big hat and some sunscreen immediately.
   D. By insulating his house with the best material available, Scott *compelled* the majority of the heat produced by the fireplace to stay inside.

10) A. Tory *abjured* all the support she had given to the coach, who, as it turned out, had been a criminal the whole time.
   B. Henry loved his brother, but he was *abjured* by the suggestion that they go shoplift together.
   C. The surgeon *abjured* any techniques approved while his arch rival was president of the medical board.
   D. John claimed to love hearing his grandchildren play the drums, even if the noise they made was *abjured* to the ears of everyone else in the room.

Lesson 5 continued:

11) A. An owner and his or her dog can have an *aegis* relationship so long as they reach an understanding of who is the master.
    B. Operating under the *aegis* of its billion-dollar parent company, the drug manufacturer rarely worried about lawsuits.
    C. Disowned, Richie no longer enjoyed the *aegis* of his wealthy family's influence and was forced to work and live responsibly, like anyone else.
    D. Judith hoped the *aegis* ingredients in her toothpaste would strengthen her teeth.

12) A. Organisms that have a mutualistic relationship with other organisms depend on a unique *concord* that benefits both of them.
    B. With the treaty signed by both counties, the *concord* between them declared that a truce was now in effect.
    C. Most people would agree that a *concord* of milk and cookies make for a great snack.
    D. When Shana arrived home, she found her scissors and began to sever the *concord* that attached the tags to her new clothes.

13) A. It took a lot of pleading, but once Vince promised to clean his room, his mother *consented* to his going to the concert with his friends.
    B. Grant *consented* that if he spent his money wisely at the supermarket, he could afford new paintbrushes.
    C. As they flew over the Atlantic, the pilot *consented* that the plane would arrive at its destination on time.
    D. Only once a hippogriff has bowed its head to a person has it *consented* to let him or her ride it.

14) A. The math teacher instructed her students to check that both sides of the algebraic equation are in *equity*.
    B. The federal judge was well respected for his *equity*; he ensured that all defendants received fair trials.
    C. When splitting the last piece of cake with his sister, Carl made portions that were in *equity* so she would not complain.
    D. Valuing *equity*, Sarah ignored each of her children's stories before deciding to discipline both for having broken the lamp while bickering with each other.

15) A. David had been *contracted* to perform two shows a day on the cruise ship, so he became upset when, at sea, the cruise line demanded he perform three shows with no raise in his pay.
    B. Having found several structural violations, the restaurant owners sued the builders they had *contracted* for the job.
    C. The chef *contracted* the servers to bring out the food when he set it under the heat lamps and rang the bell.
    D. If you wanted to keep your papers in order, you should have *contracted* them together with a paperclip.

Lesson 5 continued:

16) A. The names on memorials are recorded not only for victims' families, but for *posterity* as well.
    B. The celebrity posed for the *posterity* of the paparazzi before getting into her limousine.
    C. Archaeologists wonder if the Egyptians realized how their burial methods would be fascinating for *posterity* centuries later.
    D. The *posterity* of the earth depends on humans' ability to take care of its environment and its creatures.

17) A. The DJ's crowd cheered with *felicity* when he put on the current number one song.
    B. Karin's closet reflected colors of *felicity* and sophistication.
    C. Danny's parents were unsure of the source of their son's *felicity* until they realized it was the first day of summer vacation.
    D. The actress tried to contain her *felicity* when she found out she received the lead role in the upcoming television series.

18) A. Using leeches as cures was a common medical practice that has become *antiquated.*
    B. The relationship between the high school sweethearts was *antiquated,* but remained strong.
    C. The water filter has become *antiquated,* as it is clogged with impurities and no longer works effectively.
    D. Modern farmers shudder at the thought of returning to *antiquated* tools and technologies that had resulted in harsh lives filled with backbreaking labor.

19) A. Heavy taxes on virtually every product were typical elements of the king's *despotism.*
    B. Under the authority of the president's *despotism,* he could overrule the decisions of the Senate.
    C. For most tyrants, *despotism* lasts only until the people stop tolerating it and rebel against the leadership.
    D. With his *despotism,* the prime minister was able to increase the county's revenue by opening trade with the rest of the world.

20) A. The bookstore clerk led the customer to the section of *pious* books and bibles.
    B. Damian never goes to church, but just because he is not *pious* does not mean that he is without morals.
    C. As *pious* as everyone thought she was, her actions at the party revealed her true nature.
    D. Billy tried to appear *pious,* but the chocolate stains around his mouth proved his guilt.

Lesson 5 continued:

21) A. As the storm approached, the Greek fleet sent up their *supplications* to the gods as they readied the ship for the rough winds and enormous swells.
    B. In spite of Gina's *supplications* for a decent grade, there was a D written in red ink on the top corner of her paper.
    C. The candles and lanterns offered light when the power went out as *supplications* to the darkness.
    D. As the churchgoers filed out of the pews, some placed monetary *supplications* into the collection dish by the door.

22) A. The victim's description of the suspect was so *arbitrary* that the sketch artist could not produce anything more than a rough drawing.
    B. Even though there was not an obvious pattern, and the painting as a whole seemed *arbitrary*, the critics praised the work.
    C. The poster in the dentist's office depicted both child and adult teeth with *arbitrary* labels placed next to each tooth.
    D. The directions Nico received from his GPS seemed so illogical and *arbitrary* that he was sure he was headed in the wrong direction.

23) A. As well intentioned as it may have seemed, Danielle's comment about the model's weight came across as *vindictive*.
    B. Kyle went as an angel to the Halloween party this year; he wore wings and a mask with a *vindictive* expression.
    C. The *vindictive* athlete smiled and sincerely congratulated his opponent after the game.
    D. Xavier worried that if his new puppy did not improve its *vindictive* attitude toward his roommate, he would have to give it back to the shelter.

24) A. Angela, tired of her older siblings' behaving like *tyrants* toward her, refused to do their chores ever again.
    B. The *tyrant* of the supermarket tells her employees when to come into work and will ask one of them to mop the aisles if a customer has made a mess.
    C. Critics of the *tyrant* quickly disappeared from public life in the months following the overthrow.
    D. It was a well-known fact amongst the library-goers that the oldest librarian was a *tyrant* because she enforced the policy on overdue books.

Lesson 5 continued:

Synonyms and Antonyms

Match the word with its *antonym*.

1) repress	**A.** refuse
2) discord	**B.** endorse
3) prudent	**C.** prevent
4) insurmountable	**D.** injustice
5) abjure	**E.** faithless
6) concord	**F.** agreement
7) consent	**G.** objective
8) equity	**H.** beatable
9) compel	**I.** hostility
10) antiquated	**J.** encourage
11) pious	**K.** unwise
12) arbitrary	**L.** modern

Lesson 5 continued:

Synonyms and Antonyms

Match the word with its *synonym*.

13) exasperate	**A.** esteemed
14) aspire	**B.** vengeful
15) coerce	**C.** support
16) venerable	**D.** descendants
17) felicity	**E.** pressure
18) aegis	**F.** authoritarianism
19) contracted	**G.** aggravate
20) posterity	**H.** dictators
21) despotism	**I.** bliss
22) supplications	**J.** agreed
23) vindictive	**K.** aim
24) tyrants	**L.** pleas

END of LESSON 5

Lesson 6

Writing and Language Test

A set of questions accompanies each passage. The questions will ask you to make editorial decisions that improve or correct language, grammar, and construction errors in the paragraphs, including any accompanying graphics. Read the passage and then choose the best answer to each of the questions. In some instances, no change will be necessary.

Questions 1–11 are based on the following passage.

— 1 —

It is repeated ***ad nauseam*** that humans **{ 1 }** only typically use 10% of their brain. Fiction has responded with a **plethora** of unusually gifted individuals using 90% or even 100% of their brains. The Teen Titans' adversary, Deathstroke the Terminator, is an early example (1980), but from the television series *Heroes* (2006-2010) to the movie *Limitless* (2011), it's easy to see that the **motif** has crossed into other media. Recent movies such as *Lucy* (2014) show that this belief is in little danger of ending.

— 2 —

[1] This erroneous idea has certainly created difficulties, and its origins are uncertain. [2] The origin of the mistake is murky. [3] Some claim that Albert Einstein attributed his own intelligence to the 10% belief, but **{ 2 }** there are no documentations. [4] The idea seems to have begun around the turn of the 20th century, when scientist William James wrote philosophically in his essay "The Energies of Men" that mankind is "making use of only a small part" of our "mental **potential**." [5] Years later, a self-help book entitled *How to Win Friends and Influence People*, written by Dale Carnegie, translated James's "small part" to the **rigid** number of 10%. **{ 3 } { 4 }**

1

A) NO CHANGE
B) typically use only
C) use only, typically
D) typically only use

2

A) NO CHANGE
B) there is no documentation
C) there are no documents
D) there is not documentation

3

Choose the unnecessary sentence that could be deleted from paragraph 2.

A) sentence [2]
B) sentence [3]
C) sentence [4]
D) sentence [5]

4

Choose the sentence that, if placed at the end of paragraph 2, would best improve the transition between paragraphs 2 and 3.

A) Unfortunately, Mr. Carnegie's number was not exactly accurate.
B) Some self-help books might have been closer to the reality.
C) Nothing the brain does can be described as simple.
D) Mr. Carnegie was a writer and lecturer, famous for his self-improvement books.

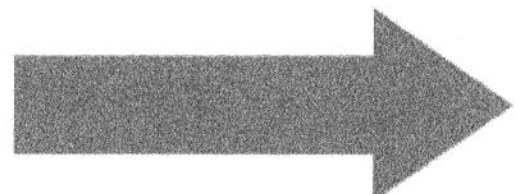

Lesson 6 continued:

— 3 —

{ 5 } Irregardless of the dumb things we sometimes do, { 6 } a full 100% of the brain is used by humans—not that it wouldn't be nice if humans used only 10% of their brains; head injuries would be far less **debilitating**. Wasting 90% of an organ that demands 20% of a human's energy resources makes no **anatomical** sense. Science should further **debunk** the myth but, unfortunately, fails at times. Just the PET (positron emission **tomography**) and MRI (magnetic resonance imaging) real-time 3D scans show 35% increases in brain activity for tasks; however, the term "activity" is misleading. Most of the scans show not which parts of the brain are active or inactive, but which parts of the brain are only slightly more active than others.

— 4 —

The idea that humans use the entire brain all the time might, at first, seem as absurd as the 10% myth. Certainly, **deciphering abstract** symbols or writing a bestselling novel requires more effort than simply sitting, waiting, or passively observing. How could our impressive brains be fully engaged { 7 } during simple activities. The answer to that question is easy: There's no such thing as a simple activity when the brain is involved.

— 5 —

{ 8 } [1] Take into mind the simple task of watching a bicycle pass by on the sidewalk outside the window. [2] The instant that information arrives in the brain, it is broken into **disparate** categories, such as color, shape, distance, direction, motion, etc. [3] These components, in nanoseconds, are compared to and matched up with stored information. [4] The resulting recombination of data is matched up to a database of compatible possibilities, and the one selected is "bike." [5] The eye receives the image, and nerves relay the information to the brain. { 9 } [6] Now, account for everything else in the scene—the grass, the bicyclist, the sky, the houses across the street, the birds, the breeze, and so on. [7] All those things are going through the same process as the bike, and this is occurring every waking moment.

5

A) NO CHANGE
B) Irregardless to
C) With regards to
D) In spite of

6

A) NO CHANGE
B) humans use 100% of their brains
C) humans use all 100% of their brains
D) 100% of the brain is used by humans

7

A) NO CHANGE
B) amid simple activities
C) during simple activities?
D) during simple activity

8

A) NO CHANGE
B) Also, there's
C) Consider
D) Think on

9

To best fit the sequence of events in paragraph 5, sentence [5] should be moved to follow

A) sentence [1].
B) sentence [3].
C) sentence [4].
D) sentence [7].

Lesson 6 continued:

— 6 —

The brain is highly interconnected. Though certain regions are responsible for certain activities, new skills are gained and improved not by harnessing new areas of the brain, but by strengthening the connections between existing **neurons**. Strengthening the connections allows faster information relays, stronger associations, and { **10** } the improvement of recognition of patterns. This explanation of the brain's "wiring" also accounts for how victims of head **trauma** are able to recover abilities that had been lost and assumed gone for good. With therapy and stimulation, the uninjured portions of the brain can sometimes establish new, rerouted connections that compensate for the damage to other areas. { **11** }

— 7 —

A 2012 survey from the Michael J. Fox Foundation showed that 65% of the general population accepts the myth that we use only a small portion of the brain as fact. The belief has no real victims except for those who fall for **charlatans** selling books or medicine with promises of "unlocking unused brain potential." Like most things, the only way to unlock your brain potential is to do it the old-fashioned way: through concentration, discipline, and plenty of mental exercise.

10

A) NO CHANGE
B) an increase in the
C) most improved
D) better

11

If the writer wanted to clarify the topic of paragraph 6, the best supporting detail to add would be

A) more measurements of changes in brain activity while subjects perform simple tasks.
B) a short explanation of neurons.
C) the logic of believing in the 10% myth.
D) more examples of misconceptions of brain function among popular culture media.

Lesson 6 continued:

Vocabulary: Context Answers

The following sentences contain vocabulary words used in the reading passage. Choose the answer that best completes the sentence. There may be more than one technically correct answer, but one will better exemplify the italicized vocabulary word than the others will.

1) Megan was talking *ad nauseam* about her rowdy children, so we _____.
   A. decided to give her some advice
   B. told her stories of our own children's mishaps
   C. ignored the rest of her speech
   D. asked her if she needed a babysitter
   E. complimented her parenting skills

2) Because of the *plethora* of options at the lunch buffet, Michael _____.
   A. couldn't find anything to eat
   B. didn't see any food that looked appealing
   C. asked to see the manager
   D. could not fit all his food on one plate
   E. ate some of his friend's meal

3) _____ can be a *potential* hazard in the classroom.
   A. Leaving the lights turned off
   B. Watching educational movies instead of reading
   C. Allowing students to study right before tests
   D. Having students sit in rows
   E. Letting younger kids use scissors

4) Colin was *rigid* in his beliefs, _____ his opinions.
   A. never thinking about
   B. allowing nothing to change
   C. always altering
   D. asking others to evaluate
   E. never staying true to

5) Casey's *debilitating* medical condition _____ her daily activities.
   A. improved
   B. impeded
   C. invigorated
   D. assisted
   E. lessened

6) The *anatomical* study of the tiger revealed _____.
   A. the big cat last ate a wild rabbit
   B. its stripes were brown, not black
   C. the animal had larger bones than expected
   D. the tiger had a grumpy personality
   E. it did not like human attention, but wasn't as aggressive as thought previously

7) The two brothers were able to *debunk* the ghostly whispering, proving _____.
   A. it was just the wind outside
   B. it was a real ghost speaking to them
   C. that the house was haunted
   D. it was not their imagination
   E. that it was a bad idea to stay up past their bedtime

8) Dr. Woodrow, an expert in *tomography*, determined the _____.
   A. painting wasn't really a Rembrandt
   B. language was based on Latin
   C. bone should be examined using an X-ray machine
   D. plants would grow better in the shade
   E. new computer would make everyday life easier

Lesson 6 continued:

9) Cornelia spent her lifetime *deciphering* the calls of eagles and concluded that _____.
   A. eagles were wonderful creatures
   B. each sound had a different meaning
   C. she was not suited for studying birds
   D. the calls varied in loudness
   E. most eagles can make only one sound

10) Although Adele and Olivia _____, they have very *disparate* personalities.
   A. are strangers
   B. attend different universities
   C. live in similar cities
   D. were raised together
   E. play soccer and field hockey

11) The *trauma* of _____ left a mark on Helen's life.
   A. seeing the highway accident
   B. hearing a buzzing bee
   C. believing the worst was yet to come
   D. experiencing her first indoor concert
   E. losing the chess match

12) The *charlatans* at the Hollywood event tried to _____.
   A. get autographs of the actors
   B. sneak around the security guards
   C. steal one of the photographer's cameras
   D. rip the actress's expensive dress
   E. pose as real celebrities

Lesson 6 continued:

Writing Practice

Each of the following sentences contains a modifying phrase that may or may not be clear or correct. Choose the answer that best corrects the sentence while retaining the intended meaning of the original sentence. Select NO CHANGE if the provided sentence is correct.

1) In the early morning, the hunter stood over the deer wearing a camouflage jacket.
   A. NO CHANGE
   B. While standing over the deer in the early morning, the hunter was wearing a camouflage jacket.
   C. The early morning and wearing a camouflage jacket, the hunter stood over the deer.
   D. The hunter stood over the deer wearing a camouflage jacket in the early morning.

2) Tabitha found a silver man's watch in the coat she bought from the thrift store.
   A. NO CHANGE
   B. Tabitha found a man's silver watch she bought from the thrift store in the coat.
   C. Tabitha found a man's silver watch in the coat she bought from the thrift store.
   D. In the coat, Tabitha found a silver man's watch she bought from the thrift store.

3) Out of the entire class, Olivia only donated ten dollars to the animal shelter.
   A. NO CHANGE
   B. Only out of the entire class, Olivia donated ten dollars to the animal shelter.
   C. Olivia donated ten dollars to only the animal shelter, out of the entire class.
   D. Out of the entire class, only Olivia donated ten dollars to the animal shelter.

4) Saturday morning, Robert ate a banana in pajamas coming down the stairs.
   A. NO CHANGE
   B. Saturday morning, while coming down the stairs, Robert ate a banana in pajamas.
   C. Saturday morning, Robert, still wearing pajamas, ate a banana while coming down the stairs.
   D. Saturday morning, while wearing pajamas, Robert ate a banana coming down the stairs.

5) The man walked into the restaurant and carried a bouquet of flowers.
   A. NO CHANGE
   B. The man walked, carrying a bouquet of flowers, into the restaurant.
   C. Carrying a bouquet of flowers into the restaurant, the man walked.
   D. The man carried a bouquet of flowers walking into the restaurant.

6) Jenny returned the books to the shelf that she had read.
   A. NO CHANGE
   B. Jenny returned to the shelf the books that she had read.
   C. The books that she had read, Jenny returned to the shelf.
   D. Jenny returned the books that she had read to the shelf.

Lesson 6 continued:

7) Claire read almost the whole book in one sitting.
   A. NO CHANGE
   B. Claire almost read the whole book in one sitting.
   C. Claire read the whole book in almost one sitting.
   D. Claire read the whole book almost in one sitting.

8) Gina saw a flock of geese on the way to the grocery store.
   A. NO CHANGE
   B. On the way to the grocery store, Gina saw a flock of geese.
   C. A flock of geese is what Gina saw on the way to the grocery store.
   D. Gina saw, on the way to the grocery store, a flock of geese.

9) Paula wore her one skirt to the piano recital, which was, unfortunately, stained with coffee.
   A. NO CHANGE
   B. Unfortunately stained with coffee, Paula wore her one skirt to the piano recital.
   C. Paula wore her one unfortunately coffee-stained skirt to the piano recital.
   D. Paula wore her one skirt, which was, unfortunately, stained with coffee, to the piano recital.

10) Eduardo agreed, next month, to visit his pen pal in Costa Rica.
   A. NO CHANGE
   B. Next month, Eduardo agreed to visit his pen pal in Costa Rica.
   C. Eduardo agreed to visit his pen pal in Costa Rica next month.
   D. In Costa Rica, Eduardo agreed to visit his pen pal next month.

Lesson 6 continued:

Vocabulary: Choosing the Right Use

The following sentences contain vocabulary words used in the reading passage. Identify the sentence or sentences that use the italicized vocabulary word properly. We have changed the form of some vocabulary words to provide new contexts; for example, some adjectives and verbs have been used as nouns.

1) A. The shellfish from the night before left the entire Miles family feeling feverish and *ad nauseam* for the next three days.
   B. We already discussed whether you can go to the beach this weekend *ad nauseam*; asking again will not change my answer.
   C. Reading in a moving vehicle makes Hunter *ad nauseam*, so he just listens to music instead.
   D. The presidential candidates' political views were already well known, but that didn't prevent their opinions from being broadcast on every TV channel *ad nauseam* until the day of the election.

2) A. I had hoped to read a *plethora* of books over the summer, but my friends took up most of my time.
   B. While the look of the car, with its sleek design and premium wheels, made it appealing enough, the *plethora* of luxury options in the car's interior was supposed to be the main selling point.
   C. After the town received a *plethora* of rain, the soil had barely enough moisture to keep the crops from wilting.
   D. The *plethora* of donations prohibited the charity from purchasing a sufficient number of school supplies for the children in their program.

3) A. What it means to be human was a recurring *motif* throughout the science fiction film.
   B. The *motif* of the rain at the end of the chapter foreshadows a change will occur for the characters in the coming pages.
   C. The romantic *motif* within the work suggests that the poet was in love during the time he penned it.
   D. Ms. Bennet prompted her class to discuss the *motif* of the main character's flaws.

4) A. The *potential* of the shack's structure could not withstand the force of the tornado.
   B. Sandy has the *potential* to be a great violinist, but she has to be dedicated enough to put in the hours for practice.
   C. Despite his training, Jim's *potential* with the weights could not surpass his competitor's own ability.
   D. The great size of the watermelon gave it the *potential* to be a winner at the county fair.

5) A. Percy was *rigid* when he came home to the mess his dog had made in the living room.
   B. When Luke gave his mother his report card, he winced at her *rigid* tone that was full of disappointment.
   C. The cat's ears went *rigid* as it listened for the sound of mice rustling in the tall grass.
   D. The new social studies teacher set up *rigid* rules in the classroom.

6) A. An afternoon of coloring had left Claire's crayons *debilitated* to stubs.
   B. The effects of sun exhaustion were *debilitating* for the tourists, who had not realized how hot the desert could become.
   C. Sitting in a hospital bed for weeks was as *debilitating* to Hal's pitching ability as the original injury was.
   D. The *debilitating* number of trees in the rainforest is concerning for environmentalists.

Lesson 6 continued:

7) A. The veterinarian consulted a book showing the *anatomical* details of a porcupine before beginning the checkup on her pointy patient.
   B. When the baseball hit their aunt's vase and it broke, the kids knew they would have to reassemble it to its original *anatomical* structure.
   C. Those who wish to pursue a medical profession must spend years gaining *anatomical* expertise.
   D. Andrew loves puzzles, and he tries to complete their *anatomical* form without looking at the image on the box.

8) A. The newspaper *debunked* all of the politician's claims of innocence.
   B. At their mother's call, the children *debunked* from the tree house and ran inside for lunch.
   C. Despite the extensive evidence, the scientist was determined to *debunk* the findings of her rival.
   D. With the child in his arms, the firefighter *debunked* down the ladder one rung at a time.

9) A. The dissected frog provided a *tomography* for the biology students.
   B. With the *tomography* of the patient's chest, the doctors could determine the severity of his injuries.
   C. Once the forensics team takes apart what is left of the car, they will have a *tomography* that will help them understand the cause of the accident.
   D. The *tomography* of the pharaoh's remains allowed the archaeologists to study the body without unwrapping its ancient burial shroud.

10) A. During the war, each side had teams *deciphering* messages that were intercepted from the enemy in order to figure out their next move.
    B. Trina is the kind of person who loves to read her horoscope and *decipher* the meaning of her dreams.
    C. After storms, my father and I would walk along the beach *deciphering* seashells, driftwood, and the occasional message in a bottle.
    D. Meredith's hobbies are mostly made up of *deciphering* stamps and bottle caps.

11) A. The lifeguards communicate using *abstract* hand motions created when needed.
    B. Charlie's *abstract* painting looked nothing like what the title, "Fish at Work," suggested.
    C. Carla sometimes forgets that her opinions are simply *abstract* ideas that have no more value or importance than those belonging to anyone else.
    D. When we asked Betty if she was feeling okay, she only nodded and gave us an *abstract* smile.

12) A. Commuters of all walks of life got off the bus and proceeded to their *disparate* jobs in the myriad buildings, stores, and offices downtown.
    B. Kelsey and her sisters spent all afternoon organizing their *disparate* collection of nail polish.
    C. When Zelda folds her laundry, she divides her clothes into *disparate* piles based on whether they are dresses, shirts, or pants.
    D. Once properly sealed, the jam jars are placed into *disparate* boxes until full and then they are loaded onto trucks for shipping.

Lesson 6 continued:

Synonyms and Antonyms

Match the word with its *antonym*.

1) plethora	**A.** rejuvenating
2) potential	**B.** concrete
3) rigid	**C.** confirm
4) debilitating	**D.** scarcity
5) debunk	**E.** inability
6) abstract	**F.** flexible

Match the word with its *synonym*.

7) motif	**A.** interpreting
8) disparate	**B.** excessively
9) deciphering	**C.** fraud
10) ad nauseam	**D.** theme
11) trauma	**E.** different
12) charlatan	**F.** damage

END
of
LESSON 6

Lesson 7

Questions 12–22 are based on the following passage.

— 1 —

In 1961, Stanley Milgram, a social psychologist from Yale University, conducted an experiment to test the conflict **{ 12 }** among personal belief and **submission** to authority. Beginning his work approximately three months after the trial of Nazi Adolf Eichmann had begun, Milgram wanted to compare the repeatedly used Nazi defense of "I was only following orders" against a situation in which a subject was **intimately** involved and free to make his own decisions.

— 2 —

Volunteers from outside the university were paid to take part in an experiment involving "memory and learning." Someone pretending to be a supervisor and wearing a lab coat managed a "teacher," and "learners" who participated in the experiment were **duplicitous** research assistants. The only test subject was the volunteer "teacher." **{ 13 }** Learners (the research assistants) were strapped into a machine designed to administer electric shocks. The teachers were tasked to administer the shocks when the learners provided incorrect responses to **{ 14 }** questions; first, however, teachers were given a mild electric shock to ensure they understood the penalty for incorrect answers. Unbeknownst to the teachers, the learners would not actually receive shocks, but they would cry out in pain whenever the teachers activated the electricity, increasing as the voltage increased.

12

A) NO CHANGE
B) wherein
C) within
D) between

13

A) NO CHANGE
B) Learners were strapped
C) They were strapped
D) Learners, who actually were research assistants, were strapped

14

A) NO CHANGE
B) questions, but first; teachers
C) questions; however, but first, teachers
D) questions, however, first teachers

Lesson 7 continued:

— 3 —

{ **15** } <u>Starting the experiment, the teacher</u> was led to a console in a separate room, away from the learner. On the "shock" control panel was a knob in which the teacher could increase the voltage of the supposed shocks being administered to the learners. The last two labels on the machine were "375-420: Danger: Severe Shock" and "435-450: XXX." Fake lab helpers read a series of words, which the learners were instructed to repeat from memory. { **16** } When teachers hesitated, an **authoritative** voice issued commands in an ascending order of emphasis, from "Please continue" to "It is absolutely essential that you continue" to "You have no choice; you must go on." And "go on" they did. The experiment ended when the highest voltage was **administered** three times or when the teacher refused to continue after hearing the prompts.

— 4 —

[1] Additional trials suggest that the number of objectors might be closer to 60%, versus 40% in the original experiment. [2] Furthermore, a quarter of the original subjects reported having doubted what they were told throughout the experiment. [3] Some did not believe the screaming originated where it should have. [4] Others admitted conducting their own experiments by discreetly lowering the voltage only to hear louder screaming. { **17** } { **18** }

15

A) NO CHANGE
B) Beginning the experiment, the teacher
C) At the start of the experiment, the teacher
D) To begin the experiment, the teacher

16

The writer is considering adding the following sentence:

> Teachers administered "shocks" when the learners made mistakes, increasing the voltage with each successive error.

Should the writer make this addition at this point?

A) Yes, because it helps establish the scientific expectations of the time the experiment occurred.
B) No, because it belongs in the introductory paragraph.
C) Yes, because it is a key detail of the experiment in progress.
D) No, because the paragraph describes the results of the experiment.

17

Paragraph 4 does not follow the logical sequence of ideas in the passage. To where should paragraph 4 be relocated?

A) after paragraph 1
B) between paragraphs 5 and 6
C) before paragraph 1
D) between paragraphs 2 and 3

18

The writer wants to add the following sentence to paragraph 4:

> The test might have provided shocking data, but the experiment was far from perfect.

This sentence should be placed before

A) sentence [1].
B) sentence [2].
C) sentence [3].
D) sentence [4].

Lesson 7 continued:

— 5 —

In the 1960s, it was believed that only a psychopath would be capable of administering lethal shocks to a { **19** } <u>stranger, studies</u> predicted only 1% of the participants would go through with it. Imagine the horror, then, when 65% of the teachers administered the full range of shocks. Every one of the 40 participants questioned the **validity** of the experiment, and every one expressed the desire to stop at some point, but 26 of them continued to the end. Even more disturbing is that the teachers continued in spite of increasing cries of pain and **hysteria** from the learners. The majority of the teachers had complied with the authorities in spite of their own halfhearted protests, hesitation, and **physiological** responses, such as sweating and nail biting, and truly feared that they could have potentially killed someone.

— 6 —

Scientists still question both the validity and the relevance of the experiment, but Milgram offers the following **assertions** about his research: Teachers were more willing to continue when the supervisor assumed all responsibility for the outcome; hearing the learners' complaints decreased teacher obedience from 65% to 62.5%, and removing the **prestige** from the institution—hosting at a community college rather than Yale, for instance—reduced obedience to 47%. Variations of the Milgram experiment showed further reductions in obedience, notably by decreasing physical proximity between teachers and learners and by planting other "teachers" to influence the conscience of the subject (see table). { **20** } { **21** } { **22** }

19

A) NO CHANGE
B) stranger studies
C) stranger. Studies
D) stranger, but studies

20

The horizontal axis of the chart (0…20…40…) has no title. The numbers refer to
A) percentage of test subjects.
B) unaccounted variables.
C) quantity of original test subjects.
D) number of experiments.

21

The graph compares results from variations of the experiment to the results of the original experiment. To help eliminate confusion on the chart, the writer should
A) reverse the order of the rows.
B) change the horizontal orientation to vertical.
C) include the specific data from the first Milgram experiment.
D) increase the thickness of the original experiment row, making it unique.

22

Choose the data column that does not belong on the chart and should be deleted.
A) Absent Supervisor
B) Hearing Learner's Pain
C) Duration of Experiments
D) Less Prestigious Authority

Obedience Ratio in Milgram Experiment Variants

Reluctant Peer Included
Absent Supervisor
Teachers Apply Electrode
Duration of Experiments
Less Prestigious Authority
Hearing Learner's Pain
Original Experiment

0 20 40 60 80

Lesson 7 continued:

Vocabulary: Context Answers

The following sentences contain vocabulary words used in the reading passage. Choose the answer that best completes the sentence. There may be more than one technically correct answer, but one will better exemplify the italicized vocabulary word than the others will.

1) The peasants lived in *submission* under the rule of the _____ king.
   A. gloomy
   B. tyrannical
   C. indifferent
   D. dynamic
   E. boring

2) We could not *intimately* talk to each other _____.
   A. in the vast, open field
   B. in the noisy, crowded room
   C. without other people near us
   D. unless neither of us were home
   E. in my car

3) Charlotte's *duplicitous* behavior caused her friends to _____.
   A. continue hanging out with her
   B. sit around her in class
   C. spread nasty rumors about her
   D. confuse her with someone else
   E. lose all their trust in her

4) _____, Nathan could not determine the *validity* of Kevin's story.
   A. Without evidence
   B. With context clues
   C. After seeing proof
   D. By searching the Internet
   E. Without a solid excuse

5) When _____, the claustrophobic traveler experienced a state of *hysteria.*
   A. the plane landed
   B. the elevator broke
   C. the rain stopped
   D. he took a nap
   E. the ship reached the open seas

6) The *physiological* effects of a nerve agent and similar chemical weapons include _____.
   A. worldwide criticism
   B. political sanctions
   C. paralysis and death
   D. changes in perspective
   E. altered routines

7) Shelby's *assertions* held no weight as long as she _____.
   A. kept spreading lies
   B. could not provide proof
   C. told her story without confidence
   D. did not want to
   E. kept repeating the same story

8) The college's *prestige* made _____ many potential students.
   A. it attractive to
   B. people talk about its
   C. admittance possible for
   D. tuition cheap for
   E. it unappealing

Lesson 7 continued:

Writing Practice

The underlined portion of each sentence possibly contains an error related to the use of restrictive and nonrestrictive clauses. Select the answer that best corrects the flaw. Select NO CHANGE if the underlined portion is correct.

1) Everyone who received an A last semester, is excused from the final exam.
   - A. NO CHANGE
   - B. Everyone, who received an A last semester, is excused
   - C. Everyone who received an A last semester is excused
   - D. Everyone, who received an A last semester is excused

2) The amazing book, that I read last week, is being turned into a major movie.
   - A. NO CHANGE
   - B. book that I read last week is
   - C. book, that I read last week is
   - D. book, I read it last week, is

3) The main race a lengthy obstacle course had been won by the same team twice in three years.
   - A. NO CHANGE
   - B. The main race a lengthy obstacle course, had been won by the same team, twice
   - C. The main race, a lengthy obstacle course, had been won by the same team twice
   - D. The main race a lengthy, obstacle course, had been won, by the same team twice

4) The bedroom that needs painting is just down the hall.
   - A. NO CHANGE
   - B. The bedroom, that needs painting is
   - C. The bedroom that needs painting, is
   - D. The bedroom, that needs painting, is

5) Labelle lives in a small town, that is situated right at the bottom of a mountain.
   - A. NO CHANGE
   - B. small town, that is situated right at the bottom, of a mountain.
   - C. small town that is situated right at the bottom of a mountain.
   - D. small town, that is situated right, at the bottom of a mountain.

Lesson 7 continued:

6) The rare watch which had been in the family for six generations had to be worth at least ten thousand dollars.
   A. NO CHANGE
   B. The rare watch, which had been in the family for six generations, had to be worth
   C. The rare watch, that had been in the family for six generations, had to be worth
   D. The rare watch which had been in the family for six generations, had to be worth

7) Candy that contains chocolate can be dangerous to dogs.
   A. NO CHANGE
   B. Candy, that contains chocolate, can be dangerous to dogs.
   C. Candy which contains chocolate can be dangerous to dogs.
   D. Candy, that contains chocolate can be dangerous, to dogs.

8) Of all my plants, the one in the corner the tall one, that has never bloomed before, is developing a flower.
   A. NO CHANGE
   B. plants, the one in the corner, the tall one that has never bloomed before, is developing
   C. plants, the one in the corner, the tall one, that has never bloomed before, is developing
   D. plants the one in the corner the tall one which has never bloomed before is developing

9) Joseph who kicked the ball into the yard, is standing at the gate.
   A. NO CHANGE
   B. Joseph, who kicked the ball into the yard is standing,
   C. Joseph, who kicked the ball into the yard, is standing
   D. Joseph who kicked the ball into the yard is standing

10) The 1957 Chevy, that many Americans drove simply as a middle-class method of transportation has somehow become a symbol of the era of muscle cars in the United States and is highly prized by collectors, who will pay thousands of dollars for one that's in pristine condition.
   A. NO CHANGE
   B. The 1957 Chevy, that many Americans drove simply as a middle-class method of transportation, has somehow become a symbol of the era of muscle cars in the United States and is highly prized by collectors, who will pay thousands of dollars for one, which is in pristine condition.
   C. The 1957 Chevy that many Americans drove simply as a middle-class method of transportation has somehow become a symbol of the era of muscle cars in the United States and is highly prized by collectors, who will pay thousands of dollars for one that's in pristine condition.
   D. The 1957 Chevy, that many Americans drove simply as a middle-class method of transportation has somehow become a symbol of the era of muscle cars in the United States and is highly prized by collectors, who will pay thousands of dollars, for one that's in pristine condition.

Lesson 7 continued:

Vocabulary: Choosing the Right Use

The following sentences contain vocabulary words used in the reading passage. Identify the sentence or sentences that use the italicized vocabulary word properly. We have changed the form of some vocabulary words to provide new contexts; for example, some adjectives and verbs have been used as nouns.

1) A. As an undercover agent, Carmen was warned not to become *intimately* involved with anyone who was a suspect.
   B. With the eerie music steadily increasing, people in the theater leaned *intimately* toward their significant other until the monster appeared.
   C. The tractor trailer passed by Sherri's car so *intimately* that she was sure it had taken off her side mirror.
   D. Wide-eyed, the toddler pressed *intimately* to the glass so that he could see the pufferfish as closely as possible.

2) A. Carson thought she had gotten away with it, but her *duplicitous* little brother had told her parents that she had snuck out the night before.
   B. When the flag began to thrash due to high winds, the captain sensed there was a *duplicitous* storm approaching.
   C. Jordan's history of *duplicitous* dealings with the authorities made him unpopular among thieves and swindlers.
   D. Although he had trained for weeks, the athlete began to doubt his skills once he saw the layout of the *duplicitous* obstacle course.

3) A. Everyone began to second-guess Mark's *validity* when he refused to help an old lady cross the street.
   B. The research assistant did not want to question the *validity* of the scientist's results, but they were so far-fetched that she decided to conduct the experiment on her own.
   C. Knights can prove their *validity* by slaying monsters, pledging loyalty to their king, and promising to protect the kingdom.
   D. In the past, the entertainment magazine has been known to publish fictitious articles, so readers must always question the text's *validity*.

4) A. At the comedian's punch line, the audience erupted into *hysteria* and continued to laugh throughout the performance.
   B. The news broadcast announcing that a new and deadly virus had begun to spread across the country sparked *hysteria* among the population.
   C. Black Friday sales sometimes prompt *hysteria* as shoppers clamor for the best deals on electronics and other items.
   D. Instead of the anger Tyler was expecting, his teacher reacted to the whoopee cushion with *hysteria* and praised his student's prank.

Lesson 7 continued:

5) A. The severity of peanut allergies varies among people, and the *physiological* reactions usually range from a swollen tongue to hives all over the body.
   B. Casey hoped that her teddy bear would have a *physiological* response to the magic spell she had put on it during recess.
   C. Jane worried about the *physiological* effects of lifelong cellphone use.
   D. After a *physiological* diagnosis, the mechanic determined that my car needs an oil change.

6) A. Jeff could appreciate Cameron's passion, but his opponent's argument did not improve when he simply repeated his *assertions* that he was right and Jeff was wrong.
   B. Based on Marcus's blue hair and ripped jeans, the class could make some *assertions* that their new classmate was a troublemaker.
   C. Jody's parents pressed him to try broccoli before making *assertions* about it.
   D. Mona produced a strong argumentative essay by stating her *assertions* and then supporting them with credible evidence.

7) A. Caroline's bike, once *prestige* with its woven basket and shiny bell, now sits rusting against the side of the house.
   B. The famous cyclist lost his *prestige* and the backing of his sponsors when it was discovered that he had been cheating since his first race.
   C. Jessica's favorite season is fall; she loves the *prestige* of the leaves and the superb taste of pumpkin spice.
   D. So many celebrities have been knighted that the honor does not have the same *prestige* it used to.

Lesson 7 continued:

Synonyms and Antonyms

Match the word with its *antonym*.

1) intimately	**A.** insignificance
2) duplicitous	**B.** publicly
3) prestige	**C.** calm
4) hysteria	**D.** honest

Match the word with its *synonym*.

5) submission	**A.** biological
6) physiological	**B.** accuracy
7) assertion	**C.** obedience
8) validity	**D.** claim

END of LESSON 7

Lesson 8

Questions 23–33 are based on the following passage.

Longitude can be defined as a coordinate on the surface of the earth that specifies how far one is east or west. Maps are relatively useless without **{ 23 }** longitude and sailors cannot accurately locate themselves in the ocean without it. While **latitude**, the position north or south of the equator, had been well understood for several centuries, no one could calculate longitude accurately until the late 1700s.

Until sailors had the ability to determine longitude, ships at sea depended on "dead **reckoning**," or determining one's position based on a previous position. This method is **fraught** with difficulties, the most obvious being that a small **{ 24 }** error was magnified each time someone takes a measurement, and these errors become **cumulative**. It also requires the accurate determination of time and speed, which is difficult when something as simple as the swelling of the wooden **hull** of a ship can throw everything off, let alone rough seas or poor weather.

Various other methods came and went, including readings based on stars, the sun, the moon, various planets, the horizon, and knowing the exact time—none of which were dependably accurate while on a ship moving through waves. Thousands missed their **{ 25 }** destinations and sank because accurate longitude was impossible to determine.

[1] On a map, longitude is depicted as vertical lines running through the North and South Poles. [2] During the Age of Exploration, when Europeans explored the sea in search of easier, faster trade routes, the need for a precise determination of longitude grew in importance. [3] Both Amerigo Vespucci and Galileo Galilei, among many others, offered solutions, but these proved either inaccurate, extremely difficult, or impractical for navigation at sea. [4] In 1714, Britain passed the Longitude Act and established an official Board that offered a reward of 10,000 pounds (more than $1.4 million today) for anyone who could devise a simple way to determine a ship's longitude to within 60 **nautical** miles. **{ 26 }**

23

A) NO CHANGE
B) longitude; however, sailors
C) longitude while sailors
D) longitude, and sailors

24

A) NO CHANGE
B) error will be magnified
C) errors were magnified
D) error had been magnified

25

A) NO CHANGE
B) destinations and sank.
C) destinations and sank, because of the difficulty of determining longitude.
D) destinations—and sank at sea because accurate longitude was impossible to determine.

26

Choose the sentence that should be relocated to the introductory paragraph.

A) sentence [1]
B) sentence [2]
C) sentence [3]
D) sentence [4]

Lesson 8 continued:

Since the 1500s, astronomers and sailors knew that there was a relationship between time and longitude, but clocks, in their infancy, were simply not yet dependable. **{ 27 }**

John Harrison, born in 1693, had been making wooden clocks since the age of twenty. One of these wooden clocks is still functioning in England. A few of his clocks are believed to have been the most accurate in existence at the time, and it was natural for Harrison to set out to solve the puzzle of longitude and claim the prize. He set a goal to develop a clock that would be accurate at sea, regardless of **barometric** pressure, air temperature, or **corrosive** salt air. The clock would also need to maintain perfect balance on a ship at the mercy of the chaotic motion of the sea. **{ 28 }** Harrison built a clock, referred to as H1, that he believed solved these issues in five years.

Harrison sailed with his clock from England to Lisbon, Portugal, and the clock performed well. The Board of Longitude ruled, however, that the trip did not constitute a "transatlantic voyage," as had been **stipulated**, but the Board did give Harrison 500 pounds to continue his development. Harrison built a sturdier, smaller clock, now **{ 29 }** called H2, indicating that it was Harrison's second attempt.

By 1741, Britain and Spain were at war. Harrison crafted another clock. The British government believed that H2 was too valuable to be allowed to fall into enemy hands, but Harrison was coming to understand that a watch-sized timepiece would solve some of the problems he was encountering. New methods of steel manufacturing and watchmaking had been developed that provided stronger materials and more accurate mechanisms. Watches, for instance, could continue running while being wound. Harrison, after another decade, developed his masterpiece in 1758: an instrument slightly over 5 inches in diameter that resembled an oversized pocket watch. The H4 incorporated diamonds, steel, a spring, and a dual-metallic strip to regulate **{ 30 }** it's temperature.

27

The writer wants to expand the paragraph. Choose the most appropriate type of information to put at this point in the passage.

A) descriptions of shipwrecks that occurred due to inclement weather
B) the reasons Harrison was drawn to clock making and navigation
C) a short explanation of how time is used to determine longitude
D) background details on the purpose of the Board of Longitude

28

A) NO CHANGE
B) Harrison built a clock referred to as H1, which he believed solved these issues after five years.
C) Harrison believed he solved these issues after he built a clock, referred to as H1, after five years.
D) In five years, Harrison built a clock, referred to as H1, that he believed solved these issues.

29

A) NO CHANGE
B) called H2, indicating it was Harrison's second attempt at making a clock.
C) called H2, that indicted that it was Harrison's second attempt at making a clock.
D) called H2; indicating that it was Harrison's second attempt.

30

A) NO CHANGE
B) its'
C) its
D) it's own

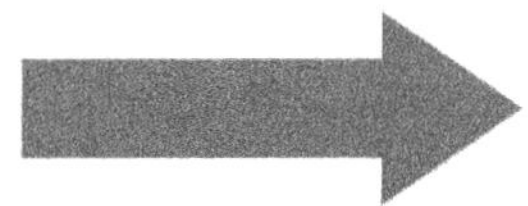

Lesson 8 continued:

The aging Harrison placed H4 in the care of his son for its first transatlantic test, during which the watch proved to be slightly inaccurate, { **31** } only lost 3 minutes, 36 seconds during the 81-day voyage. This discrepancy in time translated to a **deviation** of approximately one nautical mile. Once again, Harrison presented his claim to the Board, which decided that the accuracy might have been **attributable** to pure luck. The matter eventually ended up in the British Parliament, which offered Harrison 5,000 pounds. Upset, Harrison obtained an audience with King George III, who tested the latest version, H5, and found it accurate to within 1/3 of a second per day.

{ **32** } As is the case with any new technology, Harrison's devices, called "sea **chronometers**," were extremely expensive. It is estimated that a chronometer added nearly 30% to the cost of a British ship. Gradually, the price decreased and few ships sailed without one of Harrison's devices on board.

Captain James Cook used a version of H4 to sail throughout the Pacific in the 1770s, as did William Bligh, captain of the *HMS Bounty*, in the 1780s. Both men voiced their appreciation of Harrison's design and the watch's accuracy. The problem of longitude had been solved by one man's { **33** } intelligence, the way he was determined, and **persistence**. Parliament eventually awarded Harrison a total sum of 23,065 pounds, which he received in **increments** over the last ten years of his life. This sum, adjusted for inflation, made him a millionaire. Harrison died in 1776, on what would have been his 83rd birthday.

31

A) NO CHANGE
B) having lost 3 minutes, 36 seconds
C) and losing only 3 minutes, 36 seconds
D) having only lost 3 minutes, 36 seconds

32

A) NO CHANGE
B) As was the case with any new technology;
C) As is the case, such as this, with any technology,
D) As to the case with any new technology,

33

A) NO CHANGE
B) thinking, his determination, and persisting
C) intelligence, his determination, and how he persisted
D) intelligence, determination, and persistence

Lesson 8 continued:

Vocabulary: Context Answers

The following sentences contain vocabulary words used in the reading passage. Choose the answer that best completes the sentence. There may be more than one technically correct answer, but one will better exemplify the italicized vocabulary word than the others will.

1) Professor Brant moved her finger on the globe _____ in order to show her students the difference in *longitude* between the two countries.
   A. right onto Iraq
   B. from east to west
   C. from north to south
   D. to adjacent oceans
   E. to demonstrate that Italy is larger

2) Did you know that Alaska has a(n) _____ *latitude*?
   A. unfriendly
   B. cold
   C. northern
   D. large
   E. unknown

3) By Val's *reckoning*, the search team _____.
   A. should have chosen better members
   B. was 400 meters from the crash site
   C. needed to make sure the airspace was clear
   D. members were easy to get along with
   E. should request more funds

4) Because his essay was *fraught* _____, James definitely deserved a D.
   A. with grammar errors
   B. only the night before
   C. of a clear thesis
   D. from an online journal
   E. by an entire week

5) _____, the basketball team's *cumulative* point totals per game increased.
   A. Because they were tied with the opposing team
   B. Dependent on the skills of the other team
   C. When Josh missed three shots in a row
   D. Once the final buzzer of the game sounded
   E. As the players gained confidence

6) Milton spent an hour separating each _____ from its *hull* to prepare it for use in the recipe.
   A. potato
   B. hamburger bun
   C. egg
   D. walnut
   E. banana

7) Eric always wanted a *nautical* career, one that would let him _____.
   A. drive a police car
   B. pilot a fishing boat
   C. fly a commercial airplane
   D. own a dockside restaurant
   E. wear a uniform

8) The sudden drop in *barometric* pressure _____ meant that a storm was coming our way.
   A. in the atmosphere
   B. under the surface of the water
   C. on the car's wheels
   D. in the thermometer
   E. in my head

Lesson 8 continued:

9) Battery acid is a *corrosive* substance quite capable of _____ skin that it contacts.
   A. bursting into flames on
   B. creating static on
   C. burning or blistering
   D. glowing and pulsing
   E. causing stickiness on

10) Louie's court order *stipulated* that he _____ if he wanted the charges against him dropped.
   A. must have another trial
   B. must do community service
   C. should meet his lawyer before the trial
   D. tell a lie under oath
   E. should be at the court by noon

Lesson 8 continued:

Writing Practice

The following sentences contain words that are often misused. Choose the correct word in each sentence.

1) That lazy dog has been laying / lying in the sun all day.

2) Once Kelley finished exercising, she turned on some music and lay / lied on the sofa.

3) Setting / Sitting there in the middle of the road was a large armadillo.

4) Many people walked past the $100 bill that the TV show host had sat / set on the pavement.

5) The dominant male gorilla raised / rose himself to his full height to intimidate his rival.

6) The trumpet played softly as the soldiers began raising / rising the flag.

7) The paper airplane Hal made flew farther / further than the one I made.

8) Let's look into this problem a bit farther / further before reaching a decision.

9) The label explicitly / implicitly states that the packaging is biodegradable.

10) Explicit / Implicit in the poem is the idea that beauty must eventually fade.

11) The four teams couldn't agree among / between themselves where the playoffs would be held.

12) Among / Between both my grandparents, my dad's mom is more capable using computers.

Lesson 8 continued:

Vocabulary: Choosing the Right Use

The following sentences contain vocabulary words used in the reading passage. Identify the sentence or sentences that use the italicized vocabulary word properly. We have changed the form of some vocabulary words to provide new contexts; for example, some adjectives and verbs have been used as nouns.

1) A. Rebecca suggested they follow the path that ran *longitude* to the stream until they found a road or a town.
   B. After determining their *longitude*, the hikers calculated they had traveled too far east by three miles.
   C. The difference in *longitude* between the two cities meant that residents in one were having breakfast while those in the other were eating dinner.
   D. Hannah stepped back and made sure the bars across her balcony were *longitude* to each other before she bolted them in place.

2) A. By the inspector's *reckoning*, the cost to update the home will be more than the profit made from selling it.
   B. Depending on the weatherman's *reckoning*, the fireworks may have to be delayed until a lightning storm passes.
   C. The *reckoning* of the report summarized the events of the last few days, as well as provided a theory of what may come next.
   D. Sue thought the movie was an accurate adaption of the book, but the *reckoning* scene was where the director had taken some artistic liberties.

3) A. Trying not to drool, the children were amazed to see the table *fraught* with cake and ice cream.
   B. The expectant father was *fraught* with nerves while he paced the delivery room.
   C. Clarisse's cat is so *fraught* with fleas that she will have to get his fur shaved.
   D. The poker player was pleased to see he had a hand *fraught* with aces.

4) A. Marcy's *cumulative* hair always clogs the drain in the shower.
   B. Although Leo received excellent grades this semester, his *cumulative* GPA is still below average due to his low grades from previous years.
   C. Tourists are easy to spot because they always stop in the middle of the street to stare up at the *cumulative* skyscrapers.
   D. The *cumulative* time George worked for NASA added up to five years.

5) A. Santi claims he can split the *hull* of a coconut open with his elbow, but no one in the class believes him.
   B. The *hull* of Perry's house is in need of repair and could use a new coat of paint as well.
   C. Mastiffs and other large dogs like to chew on the *hull* of bones until they get to the marrow on the inside.
   D. The dugout floor at the baseball stadium is littered with the *hulls* of sunflower seeds.

6) A. Since Steve loves *nautical* décor, his mother bought him a model of a ship and bookends with anchors on them.
   B. Ever since Terry spent three months on a crabbing vessel, he has loved novels with *nautical* settings.
   C. The view from our beachside hotel balcony was *nautical* and relaxing.
   D. After spending a week on the cruise ship, Annabeth's *nautical* legs felt wobbly on dry land.

Lesson 8 continued:

7) A. Ethan's *corrosive* friend walked with him to school every day.
   B. Surprisingly, the sap in the newly cut lumber had a *corrosive* effect on Zach's gloves.
   C. The article on the candidate made her sound unsympathetic and *corrosive*.
   D. Acid rain is *corrosive* to statues and gravestones, so their details and dates fade over time.

8) A. Moviegoers *stipulated* that the monster would jump out just as soon as the characters were sure that it was gone.
   B. Since Ron had won the last three games of poker, it was *stipulated* that he would win the next round as well.
   C. The losing side had to buy the winning team lunch, as was *stipulated* at the beginning of the tournament.
   D. It had been *stipulated* in Grandma's will that her assets would be divided among her children, but ten percent of it would go to charity.

9) A. The strict uniform policy did not prevent Eric's *deviation* from the school's dress code.
   B. Cindy's *deviation* from the soccer team may be because she feels overloaded with homework.
   C. After the scandal broke the headlines, the mayor announced his *deviation* the following morning.
   D. The chauffer's *deviation* from the suggested route caused the GPS to recommend making a U-turn.

10) A. The success of the fundraiser is *attributable* to the volunteers who set up the carnival games and advertised the event.
    B. Darcy's car accident was *attributable* to a rabbit that she had swerved to avoid, only to hit a telephone pole.
    C. The client made the check *attributable* to the dog walker who had taken the Dalmatian to the park every day for the past week.
    D. According to her home insurance policy, Sara will be *attributable* to a large sum of money should her house ever be destroyed by a natural disaster.

11) A. The restaurant owners were unsure how they would do on opening night, but the *persistence* of excited customers convinced the staff to close the doors early.
    B. With compassion and *persistence*, Lee finally trained her puppy to stop chewing on the furniture.
    C. Max's arms were tired, but his *persistence* and desire to impress his girlfriend allowed him to continue climbing up the rock wall.
    D. We were glad when the rain came and ended the drought, but if its *persistence* continues, we may have to prepare for a flood.

12) A. The kindergarten class recorded the progress of their garden by marking the *increments* of growth on a measuring stick each week.
    B. Joan has a sundial in her garden that guests will watch as the casted shadow *increments* the time.
    C. Knowing that her hair grows in *increments*, Olivia was not comforted by her mother's statement that her bad haircut was only temporary.
    D. As Jay continued to work out, he had to tighten his belt in weekly *increments*.

Lesson 8 continued:

Synonyms and Antonyms

Match the word with its *antonym*.

1) fraught	**A.** decreasing
2) longitude	**B.** adherence
3) cumulative	**C.** indifference
4) deviation	**D.** loss
5) persistence	**E.** latitude
6) increment	**F.** devoid

Match the word with its *synonym*.

7) reckoning	**A.** casing
8) hull	**B.** marine
9) corrosive	**C.** specify
10) stipulate	**D.** owing
11) attributable	**E.** destructive
12) nautical	**F.** estimation

END
of
LESSON 8

Lesson 9

Questions 34-44 are based on the following passage.

— 1 —

{ 34 } Languages are necessarily complex; many terms and phrases from foreign **dialects** { 35 } <u>combine together</u> complex emotional experiences, and many of them do not have direct English translations. The German word *waldeinsamkeit*, for example, means, "a feeling of **solitude**, of being alone in the woods, and a connectedness to nature." *Waldeinsamkeit* originates from the German words *wald*, meaning "forest," and *einsamkeit*, meaning "loneliness"; { 36 } <u>while,</u> the English phrase "forest loneliness" does not properly express the deep feelings intended in the German term and actually sounds rather silly.

— 2 —

One interesting emotion undefined by the English language is of Mexican **descent**—*pena ajena*, which is the embarrassment you feel watching someone else's humiliation. In English, the phrase loosely translates as "other people's shame"; however, the other party, the one who is doing something humiliating, does not necessarily have to experience shame for an onlooker to feel *pena ajena*. On the subject of shame, or lack thereof, if you have ever had a full stomach, but your meal was so { 37 } <u>delicious, that</u> you simply could not stop eating, then the Georgian term *shemomedjamo* should make a lot of sense to you. The term roughly translates as, "I accidentally ate the whole thing."

— 3 —

[1] Clearly, at least some of these foreign expressions do have somewhat **relevant**, albeit incomplete and insufficient, English translations. [2] Others, though, convert to English with quite outlandish results. [3] The Italian phrase *cavoli riscaldati* describes the outcome of trying to save an irreparable relationship. [4] In English, this expression technically means "reheated cabbage." [5] Italy does not condone hopeless attempts to **reconcile**. [6] On a similar note, the Germans have another word that does not exist in English: *kummerspeck*, the excess weight one gains from emotion-induced overeating. [7] This word literally means "grief bacon." { 38 }

34

The writer wants to add an introductory sentence. Choose the most appropriate sentence.

A) Some languages have words that are difficult to translate.
B) Words that are difficult to translate include words from German, Italian, French, and Yiddish languages.
C) Words have universal meanings, even though we can't always translate them.
D) Have you ever experienced a certain emotion or sensation and simply didn't have a word to describe it?

35

A) NO CHANGE
B) combines together
C) combine
D) connect together

36

A) NO CHANGE
B) while:
C) however,
D) therefore

37

A) NO CHANGE
B) delicious that
C) delicious because
D) delicious; which

38

Choose the unnecessary sentence that could be deleted without changing the intent of the paragraph.

A) sentence [2]
B) sentence [3]
C) sentence [4]
D) sentence [5]

Lesson 9 continued:

—4—

Yiddish insults are sometimes { **39** } colorful. But usually convey something other than what the words themselves mean. *Ich zeyn dir arayn kikh* literally means "I see you in the kitchen." This sentence really does not translate well at all, since the actual **connotation** is "I hate you more than I can say," or something equally offensive. { **40** } No one understands how the idea of seeing someone in the kitchen has come to be { **41** } 100% percent **derogatory**, but such is the case.

39

A) NO CHANGE
B) colorful, but
C) colorful. However
D) colorful: but

40

The writer is considering adding the following sentence:

> The origin of the phrase is unknown, even though the phrase still has meaning.

Should the writer make this addition at this point?

A) Yes because it continues explaining the preceding line.
B) No because it should be used as an example phrase in the introduction.
C) Yes because it describes why phrases differ from single, untranslatable words.
D) No because the sentence after it already contains that information.

41

A) NO CHANGE
B) One hundred %
C) 100%
D) 100% Per cent

Lesson 9 continued:

— 5 —

A few of these terms are so universal that it is surprising that not every language has an expression for them. *Viraag*, which, in English, could mean "disfavor," actually has a much more powerful meaning in { **42** } Hindi: emotional agony from being separated from a loved one. The Hindi meaning is a far cry from the mere feeling of disapproval that the English translation provides. Meanwhile, Hindus are certainly not the only ones who have ever experienced that specific kind of suffering. **Conversely**, the French have a word used to explain the opposite but equally universal feeling. *Retrouvailles*, technically meaning "rediscovery," is the happiness felt upon being reunited with a loved one who has been gone for a long period of time.

— 6 —

Perhaps the time has come for English speakers to incorporate some new words into the language. Consider all the time we'll save, using single words to describe things that previously required full paragraphs. As long as we avoid *verschlimmbessern*, we'll be fine. { **43** }

Question { **44** } refers to the whole passage.

42

A) NO CHANGE
B) Hindi—
C) Hindi; the term describes
D) Hindi,

43

Choose the sentence that would be the most appropriate conclusion for paragraph 6.

A) That is the word that has the meaning of "to make something worse while trying to improve it."
B) That, like the other German words, has a meaning too complicated to bother with.
C) That means "to make something worse while trying to improve it."
D) Until then, we will just have to use all the necessary words.

44

If the author wanted to include another example of an untranslatable Italian word that has an indirect but understandable, funny translation, that example should be placed in

A) paragraph 1.
B) paragraph 2.
C) paragraph 3.
D) paragraph 6.

Lesson 9 continued:

Vocabulary: Context Answers

The following sentences contain vocabulary words used in the reading passage. Choose the answer that best completes the sentence. There may be more than one technically correct answer, but one will better exemplify the italicized vocabulary word than the others will.

1) Shannon's college major, _____, required her to study many *dialects*.
   A. language history
   B. geology
   C. organic chemistry
   D. business mathematics
   E. political science

2) "Did you feel a sense of *isolation* while you were _____?" asked Mark.
   A. catching up with your closest friend
   B. trying to figure out my difficult riddle
   C. in line for that crazy roller coaster
   D. at the cabin in the middle of nowhere
   E. riding a horse for the first time

3) Because the *descent* of the horse _____, buyers involved in racing were willing to pay a fortune for it.
   A. is difficult or impossible to train
   B. can be traced to multiple historic prizewinners
   C. can typically be determined by the horse's offspring
   D. is completely unknown
   E. is mainly a chestnut color

4) A question about _____ would be *relevant* at the professional-level ballet workshop.
   A. where the teacher is from
   B. a basic dance move
   C. the choreography
   D. the weather outside
   E. the best part of hip-hop

5) The two bickering friends *reconciled* _____.
   A. because one stole the internship of another
   B. that they would never converse again
   C. and went out for coffee together
   D. to sit down and work out their differences
   E. a third person for a second opinion

6) _____ has a negative *connotation* in the office.
   A. Spilling coffee on yourself
   B. Talking about the weekend
   C. The razor-sharp deadline
   D. The boss who acts rudely
   E. The term "Yes-man"

7) My French teacher found Matthew's _____ *derogatory*.
   A. botched pronunciation of *au revoir*
   B. negative comment about France
   C. sudden decline in test grades
   D. positive attitude in class
   E. constant repetitive questions

Lesson 9 continued:

Writing Practice

The following sentences contain words that are often misused. Choose the correct word in each sentence.

1) Eva's driving instructor tried to ensure / insure her that she could pass her driver's test if she simply calmed down a little.

2) No company wants to risk assuring / insuring someone who is accident prone.

3) I assure / insure you that everything will be cleaned up before you arrive.

4) The politician's newly discovered elicit / illicit conduct cost him the election.

5) To elicit / illicit proper manners in a child, exhibit them yourself.

6) Maria's Ph.D. was valuable when she wanted to emigrate / immigrate from her war-ravaged country.

7) Are there fewer / less people here than there were a few minutes ago?

8) The used car cost me fewer / less than a thousand dollars.

9) What did the professor imply / infer when she said, "Be prepared tomorrow"?

10) When it's / its over, let's go get some dinner if it's / its not too late.

11) What advice / advise can you offer me about fixing the car?

12) The rash may last for sometime / some time.

13) Everyday / Every day problems can usually be handled easily.

Lesson 9 continued:

Vocabulary: Choosing the Right Use

The following sentences contain vocabulary words used in the reading passage. Identify the sentence or sentences that use the italicized vocabulary word properly. We have changed the form of some vocabulary words to provide new contexts; for example, some adjectives and verbs have been used as nouns.

1) A. The *dialect* of the tourists was one that the guide had never heard before, so he asked them where they were from.
   B. Although the summer heat was intense, the usual *dialect* of humidity was lacking this year.
   C. Nate's parents had lived in the United States long enough that they had lost the *dialect* of their home country.
   D. The meteorologist reported a *dialect* of wind with a high chance of thunderstorms to last throughout the evening.

2) A. Hank preferred the *solitude* of the library to the loud and rowdy chaos of the playground during recess.
   B. In all the years Colleen had known her cousin, she had seen him only during small family gatherings because he preferred to live in *solitude*.
   C. The abandoned home was cluttered with the belongs left by the previous owners, as well as those who had come in and out of its *solitude* since it was deserted.
   D. Chandler navigated the *solitude* of the graveyard until he came to the headstone indicated on the treasure map.

3) A. Although similar, moths and butterflies are *descents* of each other but not the same species.
   B. Through research, my mother discovered that the *descent* of our family is mainly northern European and Scandinavian.
   C. The new car model was a *descent* of the company's top competitor and was predicted to sell better by the end of the year.
   D. Scientists believe that the *descent* of birds can be traced, through DNA, to dinosaurs and ancient reptiles.

4) A. The judge admitted that the defense made some good points, but questioned whether they were *relevant* to the case.
   B. Eugene was a dedicated snowboarder and trained until he was *relevant* to the Winter Olympics.
   C. Until the pasta is cooked thoroughly, the meal will not be *relevant* to the family.
   D. Fallon received high marks on her paper for her references to details *relevant* to the topic of her thesis.

Lesson 9 continued:

5) A. After its meal, the lion *reconciled* itself to the shade of a tree for an afternoon nap.
   B. It did not take long for the two best friends to *reconcile* after their argument.
   C. Elizabeth and her brother had always had a strained relationship, but she wanted to *reconcile* their differences now that she was getting married.
   D. The florist *reconciled* himself to his office to go over the list of needed arrangements and to order more supplies.

6) A. For those who have grown up in harsh family environments, "home" may have a negative *connotation.*
   B. A hug has *connotations* of love, warmth, and connection.
   C. Dictionaries will contain words with their *connotations*, synonyms, and antonyms.
   D. The *connotation* of a secret is an action done without others knowing or a piece of information withheld from others.

7) A. Politicians generally avoid the use of *derogatory* terms so as to avoid alienating potential supporters.
   B. Elena was despaired by the *derogatory* state of the home she had bought to renovate and sell.
   C. The alley behind the restaurant was swarming with flies, as the dumpster was *derogatory* with grime and filth.
   D. The actor's *derogatory* remark about his makeup and costume team left him without anyone to help him get ready for the awards ceremony.

Lesson 9 continued:

Synonyms and Antonyms

Match the word with its *antonym*.

1) solitude	**A.** complimentary
2) reconcile	**B.** companionship
3) derogatory	**C.** agitate

Match the word with its *synonym*.

4) dialect	**A.** associations
5) connotations	**B.** slang
6) relevant	**C.** applicable

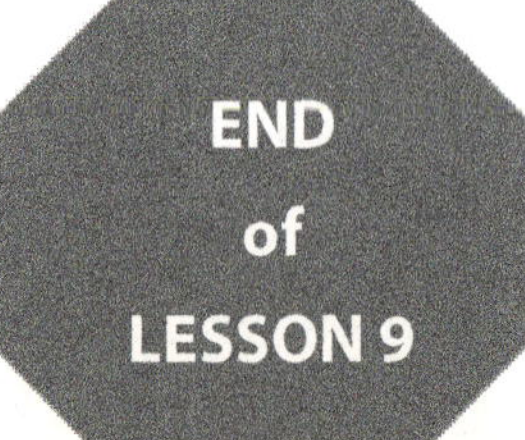

Lesson 10

Essay

The optional essay portion of the 2016 SAT allocates 50 minutes to read a short passage and respond with a well-organized analytical essay based on observations of the passage (no opinions or personal experiences—all the information needed to write the essay will be contained within the passage).

Three criteria of the essay will be scored: reading, analysis, and writing. After completing an essay, evaluate your writing using the scoring guide provided on pages 188-189.

Prompt

Choose one of the two passages from **Lesson 5** and reread it.

As you read the passage, consider how the author uses the following elements:

- **evidence** – the use of facts, examples, data, research, etc., to support claims
- **reasoning** – the development of ideas and the connection of evidence in support of the argument
- **style** – persuasive language, word choice, emotional appeals, and figurative language that add power to ideas

Write an essay in which you explain how Dickinson or Adams builds an argument to persuade his audience that America should or should not fight for independence from Great Britain. In your essay, analyze how the author uses one or more of the elements listed above to strengthen the logic and persuasiveness of his argument. Be sure that your analysis focuses on the most relevant features of the passage.

Your essay should not explain whether you agree with the author's claims, but, rather, how the author builds an argument to persuade his audience.

ASCEND

UNIT TWO

Lesson 11

Reading Test

Each passage or pair of passages, some of which are accompanied by graphics such as maps, charts, or graphs, is followed by a set of questions. Read the passage and then choose the best answer to each of the questions.

Questions 1–10 are based on the following passage.

This passage is adapted from James Fenimore Cooper's *The Deerslayer*, published 1841.

On the human imagination, events produce the effects of time. Thus, he who has travelled far and seen much, is apt to fancy that he has lived long; and the history that most abounds in important incidents soonest assumes the aspect of antiquity. In no other way can we account for the venerable air that is already gathering around American **annals**. When the mind reverts to the earliest days of colonial history, the period seems remote and obscure, the thousand changes that thicken along the links of recollections, throwing back the origin of the nation to a day so distant as seemingly to reach the mists of time; and yet four lives of ordinary duration would suffice to transmit, from mouth to mouth, in the form of tradition, all that civilized man has achieved within the limits of the republic. Although New York alone possesses a population **materially** exceeding that of either of the four smallest kingdoms of Europe, or materially exceeding that of the entire Swiss **Confederation**, it is little more than two centuries since the Dutch commenced their settlement, rescuing the region from the savage state. Thus, what seems **venerable** by an accumulation of changes is reduced to familiarity when we come seriously to consider it solely in connection with time.

This glance into the perspective of the past will prepare the reader to look at the pictures we are about to sketch, with less surprise than he might otherwise feel; and a few additional explanations may carry him back in imagination to the precise condition of society that we desire to **delineate**. It is matter of history that the settlements on the eastern shores of the Hudson, such as Claverack, Kinderhook, and even Poughkeepsie, were not regarded as safe from Indian **incursions** a century since; and there is still, standing on the banks of the same river, and within musket-shot of the wharves of Albany, a residence of a younger branch of the Van Rensselaers, that has loopholes constructed for defense against the same crafty enemy, although it dates from a period scarcely so distant. Other similar memorials of the infancy of the country are to be found, scattered through what is now deemed the very center of American civilization, affording the plainest proofs that all we possess of security from invasion and hostile violence is the growth of but little more than the time that is frequently fulfilled by a single human life.

The incidents of this tale occurred between the years 1740 and 1745, when the settled portions of the colony of New York were confined to the four Atlantic counties, a narrow belt of country on each side of the Hudson, extending from its mouth to the falls near its head, and to a few advanced "neighborhoods" on the Mohawk and the Schoharie. Broad belts of the virgin wilderness not only reached the shores of the first river, but they even crossed it, stretching away into New England, and affording forest covers to the noiseless moccasin of the native warrior, as he trod the secret and bloody warpath. A bird's-eye view of the whole region east of the Mississippi must then have offered one vast expanse of woods, relieved by a comparatively narrow fringe of cultivation along the sea, dotted by the glittering surfaces of lakes, and intersected by the waving lines of river. In such a vast picture of **solemn** solitude, the district of country we design to paint sinks into insignificance, though we feel encouraged to proceed by the conviction that, with slight and **immaterial** distinctions, he who succeeds in giving an accurate idea of any portion of this wild region must necessarily convey a tolerably correct notion of the whole.

Lesson 11 continued:

Whatever may be the changes produced by man, the eternal round of the seasons is unbroken. Summer and winter, seed-time and harvest, return in their stated order with a **sublime** precision, affording to man one of the noblest of all the occasions he enjoys of proving the high powers of his far-reaching mind, in **compassing** the laws that control their exact uniformity, and in calculating their never-ending revolutions.

Centuries of summer suns had warmed the tops of the same noble oaks and pines, sending their heats even to the **tenacious** roots, when voices were heard calling to each other, in the depths of a forest, of which the leafy surface lay bathed in the brilliant light of a cloudless day in June, while the trunks of the trees rose in gloomy grandeur in the shades beneath. The calls were in different tones, evidently proceeding from two men who had lost their way, and were searching in different directions for their path. At length a shout proclaimed success, and presently a man of gigantic mould broke out of the tangled **labyrinth** of a small swamp, emerging into an opening that appeared to have been formed partly by the ravages of the wind, and partly by those of fire. This little area, which afforded a good view of the sky, although it was pretty well filled with dead trees, lay on the side of one of the high hills, or low mountains, into which nearly the whole surface of the **adjacent** country was broken.

1

In the opening paragraph, the author attributes which one of the following reasons as the source of respect for American history, in spite of America's relative youth at the time the passage was written?

A) assumptions by uneducated settlers
B) a pride based on survival
C) oral traditions passed down
D) a multitude of important events

2

The intent of the passage is best described as

A) chronicling the comprehensive history of New York.
B) describing a vast forest.
C) establishing the historical setting of a story.
D) commenting on the politics of Colonial America.

3

Choose the line from the passage that provides evidence for your answer to the previous question.

A) "Broad belts…river" (lines 52-53)
B) "The incidents…1745" (lines 46-47)
C) "A bird's-eye…woods" (lines 57-59)
D) "the district…insignificance" (lines 62-63)

4

From lines 25-45, a reader can infer that the "condition of society" the author wishes to portray in the historic setting was one of

A) uncertainty and fear.
B) reflection and tranquility.
C) war and peace.
D) solidarity and defiance.

Lesson 11 continued:

5

The information provided in the passage would suggest that the author would probably agree with which one of the following statements?

A) It is best to begin a story with action.
B) Building suspense is essential in a story.
C) Civilization developed from chaos.
D) Forests should be cleared to allow civilization to flourish.

6

Choose the answer that best paraphrases lines 65-68 ("he who…whole").

A) A good description of one part of the region adequately describes the whole area.
B) The convictions of characters in the novel must be preserved, regardless of which part of the wild they inhabit.
C) The descriptions of single portions of the wild do not necessarily describe the whole.
D) The writer successfully portrays distinctions between different regions of the wild.

7

As it is used in line 51, the word *advanced* most nearly means

A) almost fully developed.
B) technologically superior to others.
C) moving faster than others.
D) farther into the wilderness.

8

The best description for the arrangement of this excerpt is

A) straightforward.
B) factual.
C) chronological.
D) random.

9

What words from the final paragraph best support your answer to Question 8?

A) heats, roots, leafy
B) labyrinth, swamp, trees
C) centuries, same, June
D) voices, shout, gigantic

10

Choose the statement that best describes the transition between the final two paragraphs (lines 46-95).

A) The first paragraph is vague and unfocused, and the second conveys a strong, distinct message.
B) The beginning of the second paragraph is a continuation of the thought that ends the first.
C) The first paragraph prepares the reader for the introduction of the character who appears in the second.
D) The first paragraph deals with the uniformity of the seasons, and the second with a description of the forest.

Lesson 11 continued:

Vocabulary: Context Answers

The following sentences contain vocabulary words used in the reading passage. Choose the answer that best completes the sentence. There may be more than one technically correct answer, but one will better exemplify the italicized vocabulary word than the others will.

1) Shayna's authority outweighed mine *materially*, so _____.
   - A. I chose whose proposal we followed
   - B. she chose to use her own plan
   - C. we decided to make a compromise
   - D. we decided to use my plan instead of hers
   - E. she could not argue with me

2) The local soccer teams formed a *confederation* to _____ the fields in the park.
   - A. work together to convince the county to let them use
   - B. argue about which team should be able to use
   - C. create smaller fields out of
   - D. play soccer on
   - E. show they are separate even though they all use

3) The *venerable* young genius _____ everyone she met.
   - A. was extremely kind to
   - B. complimented
   - C. ignored
   - D. intimidated
   - E. impressed

4) During the lawsuit, the car company had to *delineate* the differences between negligence and ignorance so that _____.
   - A. the plaintiffs would seem unreasonable
   - B. the cause of the problem was vague
   - C. it couldn't be held accountable
   - D. there was reasonable doubt
   - E. they seemed the same

5) Several *incursions* of the red team _____ left the blue team vulnerable.
   - A. into neutral territory
   - B. out of bounds
   - C. into their home base
   - D. into the blue team's territory
   - E. across the field

6) Kathy had never been to such a *solemn* event; no one dared to _____ at her grandfather's funeral.
   - A. cry
   - B. laugh
   - C. yell
   - D. speak
   - E. frown

7) The production delays are *immaterial* in light of the project's overall success, which overshadows any _____.
   - A. major issues
   - B. financial difficulties
   - C. unexpected concerns
   - D. significant interruptions
   - E. additional costs

8) Everyone in his family agrees that Henry's blackberry pie is *sublime*, but it is unclear if the state fair's judges will agree that his pie is _____.
   - A. unimpressive
   - B. above average
   - C. passable
   - D. overly sour
   - E. entirely perfect

Lesson 11 continued:

9) Wesley had trouble *compassing* the principles of calculus; they were _____.
   A. difficult to understand
   B. impossible to execute
   C. hard to explain
   D. easily lost
   E. amazingly interesting

10) Javier's football coach praised him for his *tenacious* disposition; he was _____ both on and off the field.
   A. agile
   B. good-natured
   C. immovable
   D. flexible
   E. quick-witted

11) Even a small cave network can become a dangerous *labyrinth* when _____.
   A. tourists can't make decisions
   B. an explorer's flashlight fails
   C. you forget to bring a camera
   D. the temperature never changes
   E. you follow the guide

12) The campsite *adjacent* to the elder couple's was noisy; they were unsure if they could sleep with all of the racket _____.
   A. in the distance
   B. far away
   C. at night
   D. next to them
   E. from their music

Lesson 11 continued:

Writing Practice

The underlined portion of each sentence possibly contains a flaw related to pronoun use. Select the answer that best corrects the flaw. Select NO CHANGE if the underlined portion is correct.

1) If anyone wants to come to the mall with Claire, they need to hurry because she's leaving in five minutes.
   A. NO CHANGE
   B. he or she needs
   C. a person needs
   D. they have

2) Mathematics are the only subject that creates a problem for me.
   A. NO CHANGE
   B. are the only subjects
   C. is the only subject
   D. are only the subjects

3) At every family picnic, either my aunt or cousins shares her vacation photos.
   A. NO CHANGE
   B. share his or her
   C. share her
   D. share their

4) Which member of the boys' hockey team most intimidates their opponents?
   A. NO CHANGE
   B. intimidate their
   C. intimidates his
   D. intimidate his

5) Raul wants to go into politics because it fascinates him.
   A. NO CHANGE
   B. they fascinate
   C. it's fascinating
   D. they fascinates

6) In the novel, each of the characters have their own fundamental flaws.
   A. NO CHANGE
   B. has their
   C. have his or her
   D. has his or her

7) Before a person adopts a parrot they need to understand the decades-long commitment involved in its care.
   A. NO CHANGE
   B. anybody needs
   C. he or she needs
   D. they have

8) Yesterday, some dogs dug holes under their fence and ran around the neighborhood.
   A. NO CHANGE
   B. its
   C. one's
   D. it's

9) At the town's festival, the number of vendor stands tend to surprise visitors.
   A. NO CHANGE
   B. tend to surprises
   C. tends to surprise
   D. surprise

10) By the end of the debate, both of the men has stated his argument.
   A. NO CHANGE
   B. had stated their
   C. had stated his
   D. has stated their

Lesson 11 continued:

Vocabulary: Choosing the Right Use

The following sentences contain vocabulary words used in the reading passage. Identify the sentence or sentences that use the italicized vocabulary word properly. We have changed the form of some vocabulary words to provide new contexts; for example, some adjectives and verbs have been used as nouns.

1) A. Jerome's hometown stores its *annals* at City Hall, to which the mayor has easy access.
   B. Meteorologists conduct *annals* in order to determine weekly weather forecasts.
   C. I am performing *annals* over the summer in the lab of one of my favorite college professors.
   D. The *annals* indicate that the Battle of Bunker Hill took place in Massachusetts in 1775.

2) A. Mr. Kline led a health *incursion* of the restaurant, making sure its owner had implemented all the new policies.
   B. Signs of the *incursion* included a gaping hole in the fence and various items missing from camp.
   C. After close *incursion*, the scientist concluded that the mold that had developed in the petri dish was harmless.
   D. After the most brutal *incursion* to date, the tribe relocated its village to higher ground to hinder future attacks.

3) A. My aunt's silly jokes seemed inappropriate after such a *solemn* funeral.
   B. Grant suggested the *solemn* idea that we have cake and ice cream for breakfast.
   C. The crowd, *solemn* in their thoughts, took a moment of silence to remember those they had lost to cancer.
   D. The most *solemn* moment of the circus act occurred when the trapeze artist flipped three times in a row.

4) A. In Jessie's latest novel, three alien civilizations form a *confederation* and prepare for war against a neighboring planet.
   B. The United States, now consisting of fifty states, began as a *confederation* of only thirteen states.
   C. Various prime ministers from all over the world met in Prague, which was hosting a *confederation* about diplomacy.
   D. Could we hold a *confederation* among all the class leaders to determine if we have enough funding?

5) A. The cat *delineated* the large spool of yarn, leaving it in a tangled mess.
   B. It took Brandon a few hours to unscramble each word that had been *delineated.*
   C. Tasha's Canadian history textbook included a timeline that briefly *delineated* each important event.
   D. Detective Farquad's notes *delineated* details from the crime scene and how they pertained to the victim and the suspects.

6) A. Mara becomes easily frightened by heights and prefers to stay at *sublime* levels.
   B. "What *sublime* work you have done!" said Jeff to his team, who had fully restored the beautiful garden.
   C. Fair skies and 80-degree temperatures proved to be *sublime* weather for a trip to the beach.
   D. The *sublime* part of the mountain gave access to the river, but the highest point of the mountain provided climbers with an incredible view of the waterfall.

Lesson 11 continued:

7) A. Though Mack is *materially* richer than Alexa is, Alexa is vastly smarter.
   B. The quilt that my grandmother knitted felt *materially* softer than the one my cousin made.
   C. *Materially*, I have a moral issue with this coat, which is made of wolf fur.
   D. We *materially* devoted a lot of time to studying.

8) A. Not quite as many people attended the benefit as we would have liked, but the event still had a *venerable* turnout.
   B. The *venerable* pope received many awards and gifts during his visit to the Netherlands.
   C. Her new entry-level job provided Tina with a *venerable* amount of funds to care for her children.
   D. The Dean of a university is considered a *venerable* position in the field of higher education.

9) A. "At this university, good grades are certainly not *immaterial*, but we care most about our students' pursuit of their dreams," said the president of the school.
   B. Unlike humans, plants are not *immaterial* beings and do not have thoughts or emotions.
   C. Delaney's perfect attendance award seemed *immaterial* when compared to something like being valedictorian.
   D. The aliens in the movie Aliens cannot speak, but they are quite *immaterial* and aware of their surroundings.

10) A. Miranda and Laurie were such close friends that they often spoke of living in *adjacent* houses so they could visit each other easily.
   B. The drawer that contains the oven mitts would logically be the one *adjacent* to the oven.
   C. The most *adjacent* component of real-life argument is to speak clearly and eloquently; however, in high-school debate, what matters is who can speak the fastest and say the most.
   D. Mr. Andrews communicated to his class the most *adjacent* ideas in the PowerPoint presentation by highlighting certain phrases and words.

11) A. Dad snapped a photograph of the church's *labyrinths* because he had never seen arches that large before.
   B. The golden *labyrinths* that stood at the front of the mansion conveyed a majestic aesthetic.
   C. The enormous library was a *labyrinth* of bookshelves that was difficult to navigate.
   D. Maureen sent her husband into the *labyrinth* of hedges after their son had not yet found his way out.

12) A. My dog sat *tenaciously* on the sidewalk; I could not get her to move, as she was far too heavy to lift.
   B. Feeling especially *tenacious*, Jana decided to join her friends who were going cliff-diving.
   C. The toddler kept a *tenacious* hold on Diana's doll, refusing to let her take it back.
   D. Daredevils have a reputation of living *tenaciously*, but I wonder if they ever actually feel frightened.

Lesson 11 continued:

Synonyms and Antonyms

Match the word with its *antonym*.

1) materially	**A.** retreat
2) venerable	**B.** unimpressive
3) incursion	**C.** cheerful
4) immaterial	**D.** significant
5) tenacious	**E.** slightly
6) solemn	**F.** weak

Match the word with its *synonym*.

7) adjacent	**A.** maze
8) compass	**B.** define
9) sublime	**C.** neighboring
10) labyrinth	**D.** superb
11) delineate	**E.** association
12) confederation	**F.** understand

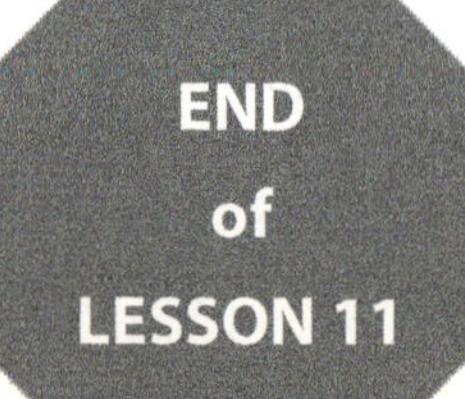

Lesson 12

Questions 11–21 are based on the following passage.

This passage discusses the history and effectiveness of microloans.

Fifty dollars might not be considered a big investment in the United States, but in impoverished parts of the world, where people are lucky to earn fifty dollars a year, that small amount of money can provide a budding **entrepreneur** with the stability and security a fledgling business needs for success. Such is the claim of microcredit organizations, which offer loans to poor borrowers who, having no job history or assets to offer as **collateral**, would not otherwise qualify for traditional loans. Through microcredit, people of little to no means, education, or even the ability to read a bank statement, might be able to borrow just enough to establish a lifeline out of poverty. A tiny loan that pays for a shelter, a hand-pump for a well, or garden tools, is one whose **dividends** pay out as a better life for the recipient and anyone in his or her care.

The concept of microcredit was popularized by economist Muhammad Yunus, who established the Grameen Bank in 1976 to aid the struggling Bangladesh economy. He went on to win the Nobel Peace Prize for his efforts. His idea of microfinance seemed **innovative** and brilliantly simple: People from **affluent**, **capitalistic** countries could donate to financial institutions that would make loans only to people the loans would help most. As microloans began to lift people out of the lowest depths of poverty, Yunus theorized, the regions would develop sustainability, slowly **eradicating** poverty and eventually rendering global poverty a problem of the past.

The bank opened with a five-part **mandate**: extend money to poor people who traditionally could not qualify for loans; reduce **exploitation** of the poor by unethical lenders; create opportunities and employment; educate the most disadvantaged citizens, frequently single mothers, in money management; and allow the poor to experience a change from low income and no savings to higher income and the ability to save. Importantly, the loans are not charity—microloans are startup money meant to elevate people out of poverty and into production, to a level at which they can pay back the money and **sustain** themselves.

For all Yunus's hopes and intentions, the microcredit model proved successful in some countries, such as its native Bangladesh, but it was a failure in others, especially when it was tried in South Africa. When Apartheid ended in 1994, the international development community made microfinance institutions a priority. Black South Africans had been excluded from the financial **sector** since 1913, and this racial exclusion increased when the National Party took power in 1948 and formally established Apartheid. Once the African National Congress assumed control in 1994, the new, post-Apartheid government encouraged microloans as a vehicle for the poor to formally participate in the national economy. The government intended to make sustainable jobs and income available to the poorest black communities and townships.

It is possible that microcredit could have been successful, but no one paid attention to how all banks were handling money. Unlike the Grameen Bank, which was founded on **humanitarian** goals, microfinance organizations elsewhere had a different goal in mind: profit. Like Wall Street investors in the mid-2000s, who found profit in selling high-risk loan **portfolios**, microcredit organizations engaged in unwise, sometimes abusive, lending practices in order to increase their profits. Loans granted at extremely high interest rates upwards of 30% ensured profit for the lender in spite of the likelihood that many borrowers would be unable to repay. What was supposed to be a relief tool for the poor class instead turned out to be a state-sponsored network of payday loan providers, or legal loan sharks.

Disastrously, microcredit had drifted from the original model of supporting income-stabilizing micro-**enterprises** to one of speculation, in which investors hoped to gain enormous returns on their money. Private banks in South Africa granted microloans to small businesses that drive neither sustainable development nor poverty reduction. The majority of microloans funded street vendors, small convenience stores, and "barrow boys," who deliver produce to the market, all of which are termed "no-growth activities." These micro-enterprises had already existed in poor communities regardless of available loans. Encouraging further competition among **saturated** markets merely increased competition and caused a reduction in wages as these small businesses became less profitable. Turf wars, sometimes violent,

Lesson 12 continued:

over business **ensued**, and the poor ended up more alienated than they were before the help.

Not only did the microloans fail to stimulate commerce—they also had to be paid back. Misadministered loans for failed business ventures leave entrepreneurs in debt. Sources estimate that forty percent of the South African workforce's income is spent repaying debt. The most vulnerable poor, who have not received financial education, often take out new microloans to pay off existing microloans for their failed businesses—a total departure from the original model of the program, in which one loan must be repaid before the next loan is granted. In addition, stronger markets **beget** more borrowing. In 2010, as confidence in the market increased, new banks applied strict rules on large, secured loans, like mortgages, which drove the poor to take on more unsecured debt than ever, and the values of microloans increased in kind.

As of 2016, the general economy of South Africa is improving. Gross Domestic Production, the value of all goods produced in a nation, has increased to $400 billion, nearly tripling in just twelve years; however, the increase has not helped the poor, as basic unemployment runs at about 25%. Economic data shows that 47% of all South Africans live in poverty, with the rate among black South Africans approaching 60%.

The microfinance industry has global administrative deficiencies, but the theory is sound, as proven by Grameen Bank. Regulations must limit unsecured microloans and ensure that institutions are not taking advantage of desperate, **destitute** people, under the **guise** of helping them. By financing education, infrastructure, and stable, income-generating micro-enterprises, lending organizations could lift regions out of poverty. In truth, microlending does need to be a for-profit institution—for the profit of the **impoverished**, not the lenders.

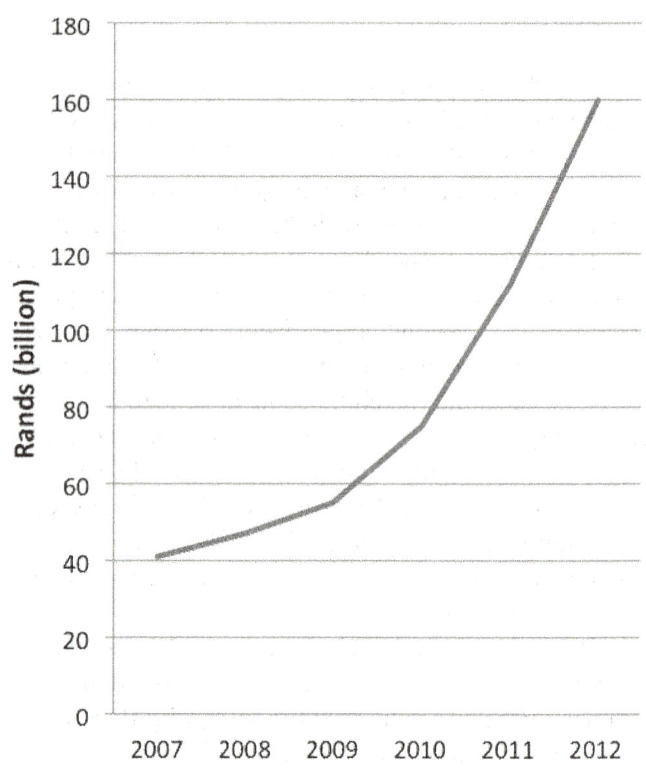

11

According to the passage, the most likely recipient of a microloan, under the original concept by Yunus, would be a

A) commercial farmer in England.
B) part-time bank teller in Mexico.
C) delivery service in South Africa.
D) homeless, drought-stricken weaver.

12

Choose the answer that is *not* one of the founding principles of Grameen Bank.

A) lift people out of poverty
B) punish those who exploit the poor
C) create more jobs
D) cater to people who can't get loans

Lesson 12 continued:

13

Apartheid, according to its context in the passage, was a system that governed decisions based on

A) race.
B) finance.
C) religion.
D) banks.

14

Choose the line that provides the best evidence for your answer to the previous question.

A) lines 101-102 ("In addition…borrowing")
B) line 30 ("The bank…mandate")
C) lines 79-83 ("The majority…activities")
D) lines 48-55 ("Black South…economy")

15

As it is used in line 22, *affluent* most nearly means

A) distant.
B) hostile.
C) indifferent.
D) wealthy.

16

As used in line 75, *speculation* is best described as

A) guessing about what will be successful.
B) investing to make the greatest profit possible.
C) cheating unsuspecting investors illegally.
D) understanding the finer details of global trade.

17

According to the passage, the failure of microloans in South Africa is partly attributable to

A) the creation of superfluous businesses.
B) the outbreak of a civil war.
C) lack of support from other countries.
D) regulations favoring nonprofit banks.

18

Choose the line that provides the best evidence for your answer to the previous question.

A) lines 96-97 ("The most…education")
B) lines 73-77 ("Disastrously, microcredit…money")
C) lines 85-86 ("Encouraging…increased competition")
D) lines 107-108 ("As of…improving")

19

The main focus of the passage is decidedly the

A) potential for abuse of microloans.
B) benefits of welfare programs.
C) abject failure of microcredit.
D) effect of first-world interference on developing nations.

20

Compared to the growth of unsecured debt between 2007 and 2008, the growth of debt between 2011 and 2012 occurred at a(n)

A) much lower rate.
B) much higher rate.
C) equal rate.
D) indiscernible rate.

21

Which event, according to the passage, explains the sharp increase in borrowing shown on the chart?

A) a departure from the original microloan model.
B) more mortgages.
C) failed businesses.
D) growing confidence in the market.

Lesson 12 continued:

Vocabulary: Context Answers

The following sentences contain vocabulary words used in the reading passage. Choose the answer that best completes the sentence. There may be more than one technically correct answer, but one will better exemplify the italicized vocabulary word than the others will.

1) _____ left the Jones family *impoverished.*
   A. The inheritance
   B. Hospital bills
   C. A well-paying job
   D. Inexpensive rent
   E. The new library

2) Sam gave the pawn shop her necklace as *collateral* to _____.
   A. prove that she was innocent
   B. keep safe until her return
   C. display as a historic heirloom
   D. guarantee that she would repay her loan
   E. sell at the flea market

3) Ben suspected that Josiah's family was *affluent* because they _____.
   A. did not buy any food for the entire trip
   B. let the boys go wherever they wanted
   C. offered to pay for him to go on the trip
   D. could not afford to send Josiah on the trip
   E. made Josiah walk by their side for the entire trip

4) The girls had enough to *sustain* themselves; they were certain that _____.
   A. they would run out of food
   B. they would have supplies left over
   C. they could get more supplies
   D. someone would bring them more food
   E. their supplies would last

5) As an *entrepreneur*, Malik knew that he needed to _____.
   A. find investors to support his new business
   B. follow his supervisor's instructions
   C. get a new job
   D. be more aggressive
   E. learn a new language

6) Officials worried that widespread chaos would *ensue* when _____.
   A. the news of a possible asteroid collision was made public
   B. the new traffic light was installed
   C. the lieutenant governor was investigated for corruption
   D. Interstate 80 was closed for two days for construction
   E. a slight tax increase was enacted

Lesson 12 continued:

7) The _____ convinced Jenna that arguments *beget* violence.
   A. calm discussion and resolution
   B. escalation of the conflict into a fistfight
   C. random, shocking violence
   D. fight that turned into a quiet reconciliation
   E. continuation of the dispute

8) The *destitute* community _____ food and clothing.
   A. had ample
   B. donated some
   C. had poor
   D. needed donations of
   E. bought a lot of

9) Manuel could not believe that Vanessa had tried to use the *guise* of friendship to get him to _____.
   A. tell her about his day
   B. drive her home
   C. listen to her problems
   D. go bowling with her
   E. betray his brother's secrets

10) The robotics club demands that its members be *innovative* so that they can win the award for _____ at the annual regional competition.
   A. accuracy
   B. speed
   C. size
   D. originality
   E. design

11) Every year, students go on a *humanitarian* trip over spring break to _____.
   A. befriend as many people as possible
   B. become more compassionate
   C. help communities recover from natural disasters
   D. have fun with their friends
   E. research different groups of people from around the world

12) If the hotel fails to *eradicate* the bedbugs, _____.
   A. it will be fine because all the bugs will be dead
   B. the few that survive will multiply, and the problem will continue
   C. it will have to try a different strategy
   D. customers will probably tolerate the leftover bugs
   E. the hotel will not be able to increase its rental rates

Lesson 12 continued:

Writing Practice

Each of the following sentences contains a modifying phrase that may or may not be clear or correct. Choose the answer that best corrects the sentence while retaining the intended meaning of the original sentence. Select NO CHANGE if the provided sentence is correct.

1) When marrying Rochelle, the entire town joined in the celebration.
   A. NO CHANGE
   B. When marrying, Rochelle and the entire town joined in the celebration.
   C. The entire town joined in Rochelle's marriage celebration.
   D. Rochelle and the entire town joined in the marriage celebration.

2) Reviewing the class notes every evening, test scores improved.
   A. NO CHANGE
   B. Test scores improved by reviewing the class notes every evening.
   C. Every evening, test scores improved as students reviewed the class notes.
   D. Reviewing the class notes every evening, students improved their test scores.

3) Warned of the dangers from an impending tornado, the sirens blasted for about ten minutes before the storm hit.
   A. NO CHANGE
   B. Warning the town of the dangers from an impending tornado, the sirens blasted for about ten minutes before the storm hit.
   C. Warned of the dangers from an impending tornado, for about ten minutes the sirens blasted before the storm hit.
   D. For about ten minutes before the storm hit the sirens, they blasted to avoid the dangers from an impending tornado.

4) While consuming lunch, a spoon dropped onto the floor.
   A. NO CHANGE
   B. While consuming lunch, I dropped a spoon onto the floor.
   C. A spoon, while consuming lunch, dropped onto the floor.
   D. A spoon dropped onto the floor while consuming lunch.

5) Reading Poe's "The Tell-Tale Heart," the main character is suffering from extreme guilt.
   A. NO CHANGE
   B. While reading Poe's "The Tell-Tale Heart," the main character is suffering from extreme guilt.
   C. In Poe's "The Tell-Tale Heart," the main character is suffering from extreme guilt.
   D. The main character, reading Poe's "The Tell-Tale Heart," suffers from extreme guilt.

6) Downloaded over a million times, I couldn't wait to see the hilarious video.
   A. NO CHANGE
   B. After more than a million hilarious downloads of the video, I couldn't wait to see it for myself.
   C. The video was downloaded over a million times and couldn't wait to see it.
   D. Since it's been downloaded over a million times, I couldn't wait to see the hilarious video.

Lesson 12 continued:

7) Understanding the need to protect and define the basic liberties of American citizens, the US Constitution included the Bill of Rights by the writers.
   A. NO CHANGE
   B. The creation of the US Constitution and the Bill of Rights by the writers showed them to understand the need to define and protect the basic liberties of American citizens.
   C. Understanding the need to define and protect the basic liberties of American citizens, the writers of the US Constitution included the Bill of Rights.
   D. After the writers understood the need to protect and define the basic liberties of American citizens, the Constitution included the Bill of Rights.

8) To satisfy the famous pianist, the movers had to place the piano in the corner of the room.
   A. NO CHANGE
   B. To satisfy the famous pianist in the corner of the room, the movers had to place the piano there, also.
   C. The movers in the corner of the room placed the piano to satisfy the pianist.
   D. Satisfying the famous pianist, the piano was in the corner of the room.

9) By discussing a great many problems, the meeting was finally adjourned.
   A. NO CHANGE
   B. After the many problems at the meeting had been discussed, the manager finally adjourned it.
   C. After the manager caused a great many problems, the meeting was finally adjourned.
   D. After a great many problems had been discussed, the manager finally adjourned the meeting.

10) Trying to take one last shot of the sunset, my camera battery went completely dead.
   A. NO CHANGE
   B. When I tried to take one last shot of the sunset, my camera battery went completely dead.
   C. My camera battery went completely dead trying to take one last shot of the sunset.
   D. When trying to take one last shot of the sunset, my camera battery went completely dead.

Lesson 12 continued:

Vocabulary: Choosing the Right Use

The following sentences contain vocabulary words used in the reading passage. Identify the sentence or sentences that use the italicized vocabulary word properly. We have changed the form of some vocabulary words to provide new contexts; for example, some adjectives and verbs have been used as nouns.

1) A. The closure of many factories in the area left the city *impoverished.*
   B. We spent weeks rebuilding the *impoverished* structures that had fallen apart during the storm.
   C. Over the summer, Talia traveled to a third-world country and provided medical care to *impoverished* families.
   D. Do you think the towers are permanently *impoverished*, or will we erect new ones one day?

2) A. Not even the world's finest mechanic could repair the *collateral* that resulted from the house fire.
   B. Danica had to use her ice cream shop as *collateral* for her medical bills.
   C. *Collateral* to the museum from the break-in included two smashed vases and two broken windows.
   D. Using Dad's gold watch as *collateral*, we were able to borrow enough money to pay this month's mortgage.

3) A. Frightened by the *innovative* noises, Alec stepped slowly away from the entrance to the haunted house.
   B. I wonder who concocted the *innovative* idea of using a potato to power a light bulb.
   C. The most *innovative* thinkers are as imaginative as they are intelligent.
   D. The mist hanging over the forest gave the scene an *innovative* vibe.

4) A. City council recently *eradicated* a new security system for the public library to prevent illegal or unsafe incidents.
   B. The camp counselor *eradicated* a number system to help keep track of all of his campers.
   C. The exterminator used a dozen mousetraps to successfully *eradicate* the rats from our basement.
   D. Jack spent the majority of the conference discussing his plan to *eradicate* crime from low-income areas of the city.

5) A. The state announced a new, official *mandate*: "Fifteen is the minimum age to apply for a driver's license."
   B. Mr. Flanders offered his students a *mandate* to help them prepare for the test: "Study the key terms and phrases."
   C. As an expert sculptor, do you have any helpful *mandates* for a beginner like me?
   D. In spite of the recent *mandate* of an 11:00 pm curfew for teenagers, many students still wandered around town well past midnight.

6) A. Always a hard worker, Mikaela *sustained* her college education by working two part-time jobs.
   B. I *sustain* my career as an aspiring novelist by working a full-time day job as a truck driver.
   C. The court *sustained* Eleanor for five years under the charges of fraud and embezzlement.
   D. Some felons are *sustained* for a certain amount of time, but receive reduced sentences for good behavior.

Lesson 12 continued:

7) A. *Humanitarian* governments often give order and stability a higher priority than they do comfort and pleasure.
   B. In college, I hope to join *humanitarian* organizations that will be relevant to my career path in social services.
   C. Some parents prefer *humanitarian* methods, caring more about grades and material success than they do the happiness of their children.
   D. One of the company's *humanitarian* goals is to eliminate old-world diseases by offering free vaccinations to impoverished populations.

8) A. Chaos *ensued* when a trio of birds flew into the dining area where the feast had begun.
   B. The weather forecast, which predicted a 95% chance of rain, *ensued* the graduation ceremony until later in the evening.
   C. The fight *ensued* shortly after the strangers exchanged insults in the parking lot.
   D. Did you know that in Australia, animals like buffalo and kangaroos can *ensue* traffic?

9) A. The film of the desert accurately portrayed the land's *destitute* span, which seemed to go on for miles.
   B. My charitable father gives a dollar to every *destitute* individual he sees on the street.
   C. Ms. Levine chose to teach the children of *destitute* families, who could not afford tutors or specialized textbooks.
   D. Seeing the Grand Canyon reminds me just how small I am compared to the *destitute* earth.

10) A. The goddess appeared in the *guise* of a poor, old traveler in order to test the compassion of the wealthy stranger.
   B. As a *guise*, Henry tied a silver dollar to an invisible string and moved it away as people bent over to retrieve it.
   C. April Fool's Day tends to be the day of the year when the most *guises* are executed.
   D. Baxter snuck into the movie under the *guise* of an employee of the theater.

11) A. "My resumé outlines the many *exploitations* I possess that would make me the perfect candidate for this job," Santos said in an interview.
   B. Some of the *exploitations* necessary for the executive director position include the ability to spearhead a project and the patience to train interns.
   C. Many people object to the use of animals to test makeup products, claiming that the *exploitation* of animals for luxury items is unethical.
   D. Mr. Banks was imprisoned after being found guilty of *exploitation* for having cheated his employees out of wages.

12) A. Would you mind walking outside to find the *sector* of that annoying high-pitched sound?
   B. The boarding school is split into four *sectors*, each bedecked with artwork thematic of bravery, intelligence, kindness, or honesty.
   C. After working as an accountant for four years, Arthur decided he wanted to leave the financial *sector* of the oil industry to become a firefighter.
   D. The *sector* of the delicious smell was not the kitchen, but next door; the neighbors were having a barbecue.

Lesson 12 continued:

Synonyms and Antonyms

Match the word with its *antonym*.

1) impoverished	**A.** preface
2) affluent	**B.** poor
3) sustain	**C.** traditional
4) ensue	**D.** destroy
5) beget	**E.** hinder
6) innovative	**F.** wealthy

Match the word with its *synonym*.

7) entrepreneur	**A.** insurance
8) guise	**B.** founder
9) collateral	**C.** barren
10) humanitarian	**D.** eliminate
11) destitute	**E.** mask
12) eradicate	**F.** charitable

END
of
LESSON 12

Lesson 13

Questions 22–32 are based on the following passage.

The following passage is adapted from President Thomas Jefferson's 1803 Letter to Congress.

As the **continuance** of the act for establishing trading houses with the Indian tribes will be under the consideration of the Legislature at its present session, I think it my duty to communicate the views which have guided me in the execution of that act, in order that you may decide on the policy of continuing it, in the present or any other form, or discontinue it altogether, if that shall, on the whole, seem most for the public good.

The Indian tribes residing within the limits of the United States, have, for a considerable time, been growing more and more uneasy at the constant **diminution** of the territory they occupy, although **effected** by their own voluntary sales: and the policy has long been gaining strength with them, of refusing absolutely all further sale, on any conditions; insomuch that, at this time, it hazards their friendship, and excites dangerous jealousies and perturbations in their minds to make any overture for the purchase of the smallest portions of their land....In order peaceably to counteract this policy of theirs, and to provide an extension of territory which the rapid increase of our numbers will call for, two measures are deemed **expedient**. First: to encourage them to abandon hunting, to apply to the raising stock, to agriculture and domestic manufacture, and thereby prove to themselves that less land and labor will maintain them in this, better than in their former mode of living. The extensive forests necessary in the hunting life, will then become useless, and they will see advantage in exchanging them for the means of improving their farms, and of increasing their **domestic** comforts. Secondly: to multiply trading houses among them, and place within their reach those things which will contribute more to their domestic comfort, than the possession of extensive, but **uncultivated** wilds. Experience and reflection will develop to them the wisdom of exchanging what they can spare and what we want, for what we can spare and what they want. In leading them to agriculture, to manufactures, and civilization; in bringing together their and our settlements, and in preparing them ultimately to participate in the benefits of our governments, I trust and believe we are acting for their greatest good. At these trading houses, we have pursued the **principles** of the act of Congress, which directs that the commerce shall be carried on liberally, and requires only that the **capital** stock shall not be **diminished**. We consequently undersell private traders, foreign and domestic, drive them from the competition; and thus, with the good will of the Indians, rid ourselves of a description of men who are constantly **endeavoring** to excite in the Indian mind suspicions, fears, and irritations towards us.

While the extension of the public commerce among the Indian tribes, may deprive of that source of profit such of our citizens as are engaged in it, it might be worthy the attention of Congress, in their care of individual as well as of the general interest, to point, in another direction, the enterprise of these citizens, as profitably for themselves, and more usefully for the public. It is, however, understood, that the country on that [Mississippi] river is inhabited by numerous tribes, who furnish great supplies of furs and **peltry** to the trade of another nation, carried on in a high latitude, through an infinite number of **portages** and lakes, shut up by ice through a long season. The **commerce** on that line could bear no competition with that of the Missouri, traversing a moderate climate, offering according to the best accounts, a continued navigation from its source, and possibly with a single portage, from the Western Ocean...An intelligent officer, with ten or twelve chosen men, fit for the enterprise, and willing to undertake it, taken from our posts, where they may be spared without inconvenience, might explore the whole line, even to the Western Ocean, have conferences with the natives on the subject of commercial **intercourse**, get admission among them for our traders, as others are admitted, agree on convenient deposits for an interchange of articles, and return with the information acquired, in the course of two summers. Their arms and **accoutrements**, some instruments of observation, and light and cheap presents for the Indians, would be all the **apparatus** they could carry, and with an expectation of a soldier's portion of land on their return, would constitute the whole expense. Their pay would be going on, whether here or there.

While other civilized nations have encountered great expense to enlarge the boundaries of knowledge by undertaking voyages of discovery, and for other literary purposes, in various parts and directions, our nation seems to owe to the same object, as well as to

Lesson 13 continued:

its own interests, to explore this, the only line of easy communication across the continent, and so directly traversing our own part of it. The interests of commerce place the **principal** object within the constitutional powers and care of Congress, and that it should incidentally advance the geographical knowledge of our own continent, cannot be but an additional **gratification**. The nation claiming the territory, regarding this as a literary pursuit, which is in the habit of permitting within its **dominions**, would not be disposed to view it with jealousy, even if the expiring state of its interests there did not render it a matter of indifference. The **appropriation** of two thousand five hundred dollars, "for the purpose of extending the external commerce of the United States," while understood and considered by the Executive as giving the legislative **sanction**, would cover the undertaking from notice, and prevent the obstructions which interested individuals might otherwise previously prepare in its way.

22

Jefferson's intent in the first paragraph is most accurately summarized as

A) an explanation of his plan for exploration.
B) a discussion about commerce with Native Americans.
C) a demand for Congress to act against poachers.
D) an introduction to the letter from the Western Territory.

23

Choose the intended audience of this passage.

A) pioneers settling in the West
B) exploitative traders
C) government officials
D) the Native Americans

24

Both of the major tenets of Jefferson's plan, as described in paragraph 2 (lines 9-51), have the mutual goal of

A) bringing peace to the Western trade passages.
B) obtaining the dwindling lands owned by Native Americans.
C) dishonoring the unscrupulous traders while exploiting their talents.
D) causing infighting among the many tribes to the West.

25

The best meaning for the word *diminution* as it is used in line 12 is

A) shrinkage.
B) growth.
C) drought.
D) sale.

Lesson 13 continued:

26

Choose the line that most accurately paraphrases the following statement from the passage (lines 46-51):

> We consequently undersell private traders, foreign and domestic, drive them from the competition; and thus, with the good will of the Indians, rid ourselves of a description of men who are constantly endeavoring to excite in the Indian mind suspicions, fears, and irritations towards us.

A) We will allow the Indians to pay the inflated prices for goods charged by private vendors, rendering them paranoid and distrustful of the government's competitors.
B) By promoting private trading, we will keep Indians happy and send unwanted merchandise to the West.
C) We will charge less than private merchants charge the Indians and, in doing so, drive the merchants out of business and maintain goodwill with the Indians.
D) Through changes to trade regulations, Indians will be free to establish their own businesses and engage in international trade with American allies abroad.

27

What benefit would the tribes receive from relying on agriculture, according to Jefferson?
A) better trade
B) less competition
C) less work
D) larger forest lands

28

When Jefferson writes that tribes along the Mississippi River "furnish great supplics of furs and peltry to the trade of another nation," the other nation he refers to is most likely
A) the West.
B) another tribe.
C) Mexico.
D) Canada.

29

Choose the lines that provide the best evidence for your answer to the previous question.
A) lines 46-48 ("We consequently…competition")
B) lines 52-59 ("While the…public")
C) lines 62-64 ("another nation…season")
D) lines 78-81 ("Their arms…carry")

30

The best meaning for the word *enterprise* as it is used in line 70 is
A) punishment.
B) trade.
C) reward.
D) mission.

31

Jefferson offers all of the following justifications to bolster his argument that the United States should expand its boundaries EXCEPT
A) other nations have done it.
B) it would be expensive.
C) the US needs the territory for trade.
D) the US population is expanding.

32

Based on the information in his letter to Congress, which one of the following statements would Jefferson probably agree with?
A) Surveying the West will be prohibitively expensive.
B) Dealing with the tribes' problems hinders expansion.
C) The US must expand, regardless of how Native Americans are affected.
D) New US trading houses will not improve trading in the East.

Lesson 13 continued:

Vocabulary: Context Answers

The following sentences contain vocabulary words used in the reading passage. Choose the answer that best completes the sentence. There may be more than one technically correct answer, but one will better exemplify the italicized vocabulary word than the others will.

1) The *continuance* of Gregor's deployment meant that he would _____.
   A. be home sooner than planned
   B. leave the military
   C. miss his daughter's birthday
   D. return on time
   E. change location

2) _____ allowed for a *diminution* of both Amy's guilt and her sentence.
   A. Keeping the crime a secret
   B. Lying in court
   C. Talking to a lawyer
   D. Being hostile in court
   E. Admitting her role in the crime

3) The cornfield _____, so it was left *uncultivated* this year.
   A. was overgrown
   B. needed a break
   C. was already planted
   D. was ready to plant
   E. was tilled

4) The presidential task force's primary concerns were *domestic*, but some issues were also related to _____.
   A. financial problems
   B. environmental regulation
   C. international policy
   D. small business owners
   E. genetically modified organisms

5) John asked the doctor if his scar had *diminished* since his last appointment; he did not want _____.
   A. to have it forever
   B. it to disappear
   C. to know where it was
   D. it to look different
   E. to see it

6) *Endeavoring* to please his mother, Lee _____, including the dishes.
   A. refused to do his chores
   B. did everything she asked
   C. did everything incorrectly
   D. broke everything in the kitchen
   E. did his chores as he normally would

7) A new law allowed *commerce* to continue, despite the _____.
   A. offensive advertisement
   B. newly elected official's influence
   C. changes in leadership
   D. water shortage
   E. lack of paper currency

8) The principal's new *sanction* _____ students to leave campus for lunch.
   A. encouraged
   B. forbid
   C. required
   D. allowed
   E. prohibited

Lesson 13 continued:

9) *Accoutrements* such as kitchen supplies and camping _____ are required for the excursion.
   A. knowledge
   B. equipment
   C. experience
   D. clothes
   E. familiarity

10) Antonio enjoyed the *gratification* of his project's winning second place at the science fair, but he was already _____.
   A. bored with the idea
   B. upset that it had failed
   C. resigned to losing
   D. angry with the other contestants
   E. pleased that it helped others

11) Mrs. Fitzpatrick's and Mrs. Markovich's *dominions* were very dissimilar; their _____ were completely different.
   A. hairstyles
   B. curricula
   C. classrooms
   D. lunches
   E. home decorations

12) The new project was slated to _____ upon the city council's successful *appropriation* of new funds.
   A. stop
   B. begin
   C. fail
   D. succeed
   E. end

Lesson 13 continued:

Writing Practice

Some of the following sentences are fragments, comma splices, or run-ons. Choose the answer that best corrects the sentence while retaining the intended meaning of the original sentence. Select NO CHANGE if the provided sentence is correct.

1) Kathryn's house, which had sustained damage to the roof, the windows, and even the pristine hardwood floors after the tornado hit.
   A. NO CHANGE
   B. After the tornado hit, Kathryn's house would require months of repair; it had sustained damage to the roof, the windows, and even the pristine hardwood floors.
   C. After the tornado hit Kathryn's house which had sustained damage to the roof, the windows, and even the pristine hardwood floors.
   D. After the tornado hit, Kathryn's house, which had sustained damage to the roof, the windows, and even the pristine hardwood floors.

2) When we finally made it to the top of the mountain after hiking for six hours. The guide helped us.
   A. NO CHANGE
   B. After hiking for six hours we made it to the top of the mountain the guide was proud.
   C. Because the guide helped us, we finally made it to the top of the mountain after hiking six hours.
   D. The guide led us to the top of the mountain; after six hours that it took.

3) Gregory won't be able to finish his history paper tonight his soccer game went into overtime.
   A. NO CHANGE
   B. Gregory won't be able to finish his history paper tonight because his soccer game went into overtime.
   C. Gregory won't be able to finish his history paper tonight, his soccer game went into overtime.
   D. Gregory won't be able to finish his history paper tonight his soccer game went into overtime was the reason.

4) I called the pizza shop to place an order for delivery over an hour ago the food still hasn't arrived.
   A. NO CHANGE
   B. I called the pizza shop to place an order for delivery over an hour ago; the food still hasn't arrived.
   C. I called the pizza shop to place an order for delivery over an hour ago, the food still hasn't arrived.
   D. Despite having called the pizza shop to place an order for delivery over an hour ago: the food still hasn't arrived.

Lesson 13 continued:

5) Mariana immigrated to the US when she was little, she learned English quickly because she lived with her grandmother, who was fluent in the language.
   A. NO CHANGE
   B. Mariana immigrated to the US when she was little and she learned English quickly because she lived with her grandmother who was fluent in the language.
   C. When she was little, Mariana immigrated to the US, she learned English quickly because she lived with her grandmother, who was fluent in the language.
   D. Mariana immigrated to the US when she was little. She learned English quickly because she lived with her grandmother, who was fluent in the language.

6) Because many of the animals in the desert depend on the few drops of rain that falls or dew that collects on the sand.
   A. NO CHANGE
   B. Life is difficult for many of the animals living in the desert because survival depends on the few drops of rain that fall or dew that collects on the sand.
   C. Even though many of the animals in the desert depend on the few drops of rain that fall or dew that collects on the sand.
   D. Whether many of the animals in the desert depend on the few drops of rain that fall or dew that collects on the sand; it's hard to survive.

7) Blearily rubbing her eyes and wishing she didn't have to leave her warm bed, Morgan got up at sunrise because she had to drive to an early job interview.
   A. NO CHANGE
   B. Blearily rubbing her eyes, and wishing she didn't have to leave her warm bed; Morgan got up at sunrise because she had to drive to an early job interview.
   C. Blearily rubbing her eyes and wishing she didn't have to leave her warm bed, Morgan got up at sunrise, this was because she had to drive to an early job interview.
   D. Morgan had to drive to an early job interview, she got up at sunrise, blearily rubbing her eyes and wishing she didn't have to leave her warm bed.

8) Regardless that I am so sick that I cannot stop sneezing and coughing.
   A. NO CHANGE
   B. Despite the fact that I am so sick, that I cannot stop sneezing and coughing.
   C. I am so sick that I cannot stop sneezing and coughing. Despite the fact that I took the medicine.
   D. Even though I am so sick that I cannot stop sneezing and coughing, I will go to school for my final exam.

Lesson 13 continued:

9) The expertise of award-winning chef Pete Zha who had studied how to create the finest dishes in Europe.
   A. NO CHANGE
   B. Learning from the expertise of award-winning chef Pete Zha who had studied how to create the finest dishes in Europe.
   C. The expertise of award-winning chef Pete Zha, who had studied how to create the finest dishes in Europe, impressed many cooks.
   D. The expertise of award-winning chef, Pete Zha, who had studied how to create the finest dishes in Europe and had his own cooking show.

10) The US won the men's ice hockey Olympics semifinal against the much more experienced USSR team the 1980 match was dubbed the "Miracle on Ice."
   A. NO CHANGE
   B. Against the much more experienced USSR team, the US men's ice hockey Olympic team won the semifinals, the 1980 match was dubbed the "Miracle on Ice."
   C. The US won the men's ice hockey Olympics semifinals against the much more experienced USSR team; the 1980 match was dubbed the "Miracle on Ice."
   D. Because the US won the men's ice hockey Olympics semifinals against the much more experienced USSR team; the 1980 match was dubbed the "Miracle on Ice."

11) The rare giant squid studied by scientists in its natural habitat hundreds of feet below the ocean's surface.
   A. NO CHANGE
   B. Studied by scientists, the rare giant squid in its natural habitat hundreds of feet below the ocean's surface.
   C. Scientists studied the rare giant squid; in its natural habitat hundreds of feet below the ocean's surface.
   D. Scientists studied the rare giant squid in its natural habitat hundreds of feet below the ocean's surface.

12) Before Lillian, who is fair skinned, went to the beach, her brother told her that the sun is harsh put on some sunscreen.
   A. NO CHANGE
   B. Before Lillian, who is fair skinned, went to the beach, her brother told her that the sun is harsh, so she should put on some sunscreen.
   C. Before Lillian, who is fair skinned, went to the beach; her brother told her, "The sun is harsh put on some sunscreen."
   D. Before fair-skinned Lillian went to the beach, her brother told her that the sun is harsh, she should put on some sunscreen.

Lesson 13 continued:

13) Gerald's father, who had spent his entire adult life in the Marines, serving in Afghanistan, Iraq, and other areas around the Persian Gulf.

A. NO CHANGE
B. Gerald's father had spent his entire adult life in the Marines, serving in Afghanistan, Iraq, and other areas around the Persian Gulf.
C. Gerald's father, who had spent his entire adult life in the Marines. Served in Afghanistan, Iraq, and other areas around the Persian Gulf.
D. Gerald's father who had spent his entire life in the Marines serving in Afghanistan, Iraq, and other areas around the Persian Gulf.

14) Tyler searched for hours for his keys before finding them in the dog crate Coco had taken them.

A. NO CHANGE
B. Tyler's keys were found in Coco's dog crate; after searching for hours and never finding them.
C. After searching for hours, Tyler found his keys in Coco's dog crate; she had taken them.
D. In Coco's dog crate. Tyler could not find his keys until he remembered Coco had played with them.

15) I was in need of fresh air, so I ran along the path in the woods that led to the lake.

A. NO CHANGE
B. I ran along the path in the woods; needing to stretch my legs and breathe fresh air.
C. The path through the woods that led to the lake. I ran along it to get exercise.
D. Fresh air was what I needed, so I ran along the path in the woods it led the lake.

Lesson 13 continued:

Vocabulary: Choosing the Right Use

The following sentences contain vocabulary words used in the reading passage. Identify the sentence or sentences that use the italicized vocabulary word properly. We have changed the form of some vocabulary words to provide new contexts; for example, some adjectives and verbs have been used as nouns.

1) A. The hours of *continuance* of Paul's Taco Shack will soon be changing from 9:00 am to 10:00 am.
   B. The manual included in the packaging of the elliptical outlined detailed instructions of the *continuance* of the equipment.
   C. Any financial donation going toward the *continuance* of the music program would be sincerely appreciated.
   D. The *continuance* of the production of this Broadway show depends on how many tickets are sold in the next couple of months.

2) A. I hope that my staying up late to finish *To Kill a Mockingbird* does not negatively *effect* my performance in the group presentation.
   B. Leila won the Nobel Peace Prize for successfully *effecting* positive change in the way her country provides education.
   C. Because his college did not offer an Asian Studies major, Finn, with the help of the department, *effected* a new course of study and convinced the dean to approve it.
   D. Do you think that the amount of makeup you wear *effects* the intensity of your acne?

3) A. "If you could return my phone call right away, please do so, as this matter is quite *expedient*," said Melinda.
   B. You should ask Marlene for guidance; after all, she is considered "the *expedient* one" in our group.
   C. The summer camp infirmary operates every day between 7:00 am to 7:00 pm, but there is always an on-call nighttime nurse in case of an *expedient* situation.
   D. The most *expedient* route is, in fact, straight down I-95, but I prefer the scenic route, which will add one hour to the overall trip.

4) A. Once *uncultivated*, Roger's land now flourishes with beans, corn, and pumpkins owing to his uncle's advice and some borrowed equipment.
   B. Most children are blissfully *uncultivated* of the evil that exists in the world and become informed only once they grow older.
   C. Your backyard will likely remain *uncultivated* unless you incorporate high-quality fertilizer.
   D. The speaker continued with his proposal, *uncultivated* of the huge piece of broccoli stuck in his teeth.

Lesson 13 continued:

5) A. The most well-known *principle* of the Declaration of Independence is the inalienable right to life, liberty, and the pursuit of happiness.
   B. "Violence of any kind will not be tolerated in school; any student who prompts violence will receive a strict *principle*," said Ms. Creant.
   C. Mr. Eckman described the cult's founding *principle* as "sincerity in its truest form."
   D. If I were to arrive home past curfew, my most likely *principle* would be "no television for a month."

6) A. We noticed the lightning's *diminishing* of the night sky and pulled to the side of the road and waited for the storm to pass.
   B. "When we enter the forest, you should *diminish* your lantern so that we can see the path well," the ranger said.
   C. Car airbags do not necessarily prevent injury, but they do *diminish* the damage that might occur in the event of an accident.
   D. "The fact that you apologized does not truly *diminish* the hurt that your insults inflicted upon me," said Frances.

7) A. Ben saved money to buy hiking *accoutrements* such as a new GPS and a lightweight water purification system.
   B. The *accoutrements* from France and Germany arrived late to the international conference.
   C. Dory and Russell, the class *accoutrements*, attended a meeting with the principal, vice principal, and superintendent.
   D. The banker wore a well-fitted suit of modest quality, but his *accoutrements* appeared to be of the highest quality, if his $10,000 watch was any indication.

8) A. Xavier found the Honor Society to be too *principal* with its restrictions on his schedule.
   B. The *principal* concern of the theme park's public safety department is accident prevention.
   C. Though she enjoys theater, going to law school prevails as Lindsey's *principal* goal.
   D. "Would you consider Ms. Lina to be a *principal* dance teacher, or does she cut you a break every once in a while?" Sheila asked.

9) A. While Teri seeks *gratification* through yoga, Benny finds pleasure in shopping for candles.
   B. "Nothing feels better than the sheer *gratification* of giving to those in need!" Jeff exclaimed.
   C. On Halloween, none of the children demonstrated *gratification*; they each took only one candy from each house.
   D. "You must resist *gratification* and simply be appreciative of what you had," said the mother to her child, who was begging for another toy.

Lesson 13 continued:

10) A. Factory workers statewide formed a *dominion* to advocate for better pay and shorter hours.
    B. Fifty states and sixteen territories fall within the *dominion* of the United States of America.
    C. Chair Warehouse and Desk City established a *dominion* and sold desks and chairs as one product.
    D. In this year's bestselling novel, a spacefaring royal family battles a rebellion throughout its intergalactic *dominion*.

11) A. The school board approved the *appropriation* of funds to pay for additional snow removal services during a harsh winter.
    B. Sonia ran for mayor using the *appropriation* that she would reduce sales tax throughout the city.
    C. The senator shamed other legislators who engage in "pork barrel spending," which involves the *appropriation* of funds for the purpose of purchasing votes.
    D. The presidential candidate's *appropriation*—"Improve Education for All!"—resonated deeply with teachers all over the nation.

12) A. After months of *endeavoring* to beat the last level, Maurice finally completed the video game.
    B. Mom tried *endeavoring* me to join her in her aerobics class by outlining the many benefits of daily exercise.
    C. The advertising company *endeavored* me to test run its product by promising me a monetary reward.
    D. The archaeologist *endeavored* for years to discover prehistoric bones in the Sahara Desert.

Lesson 13 continued:

Synonyms and Antonyms

Match the word with its *antonym*.

1)	endeavor	**A.**	heighten
2)	diminish	**B.**	flourishing
3)	domestic	**C.**	end
4)	uncultivated	**D.**	addition
5)	continuance	**E.**	foreign
6)	diminution	**F.**	abandon

Match the word with its *synonym*.

7)	appropriation	**A.**	business
8)	commerce	**B.**	equipment
9)	gratification	**C.**	fulfillment
10)	accoutrement	**D.**	jurisdiction
11)	dominion	**E.**	funds
12)	sanction	**F.**	regulation

END
of
LESSON 13

Lesson 14

Questions 33–42 are based on the following passage.

This passage describes a type of sleep phenomena called hypnic jerks.

Approximately 70% of people experience a fascinating, albeit alarming, sleep **phenomenon** called a hypnic jerk, named in reference to what is called a "hypnagogic state," or the transitional stage between being awake and being asleep. Hypnic jerks, most common in children, involve an involuntary lurch of the muscles as an individual is falling asleep and usually induce a sudden panicked or frightened feeling within that person, causing him or her to wake with a start.

Though many incidents of hypnic jerks go unremembered, they often accompany other common sleep-related sensations. For instance, those who experience jerks may also experience hallucinations, feelings of an **ominous** presence in the room, or even imagined noises or voices. These mind tricks usually **incite** a brief but startling fear within the person, which jerks him or her rudely back into consciousness. Hypnic jerks also tend to occur alongside the sensation of falling while in a dream, one of the most reported types of dreams. Usually, dreaming individuals who perceive themselves stumbling or falling feel a hypnic jerk just before or at the moment of impact with the ground. Sometimes, these visions exemplify the concept of dream incorporation, in which stimuli external to the dreamer—a noise, a physical sensation, a conversation within earshot—becomes assimilated into a dream. Essentially, the dreaming brain is thought to generate a plausible explanation (within the dream) for the real-life disturbance. In this situation, it is possible that hypnic jerks are reactions to hints of waking life intruding upon the world of a dream.

Many dream researchers believe that dreams of falling indicate real feelings of insecurity, failure, loss of control, or other obvious negative thoughts in the dreamer's mind. Research identifies emotional stress or **deterioration** as one of the stimuli causing hypnic jerks to occur more frequently. A high intake of caffeine, prolonged sleep **deprivation**, or participation in strenuous activities in the evenings, like sports or **aerobics**, also contribute to the frequency of hypnic jerks. It follows, then, that some ways to reduce incidents of hypnic jerks include cutting back on caffeine, maintaining a proper sleep schedule, and incorporating relaxation exercises into bedtime routines.

Although there is not yet a confirmed explanation for hypnic jerks, the scientific community has produced several theories. One hypothesis suggests that the twitches are actually a natural component of the human body's switch from awake to asleep. Human consciousness—or lack thereof—is controlled by two contrasting systems. The first, the **reticular** activating system (RAS), lies below the **cortex** in the part of the brain that controls involuntary **autonomic** actions, like breathing or blinking. When this system is active, the individual is awake and alert. The second system is the ventrolateral preoptic **nucleus**, or VLPO, located on the bottom edge of the brain. The VLPO enforces **lethargy**, dictating the human sleep cycle. Only one of the two systems can be in total control at any given time, and, according to some sleep-specialist physicians, hypnic jerks happen as a result of some remaining energy bursts from the RAS as the VLPO begins to assert its power over the body.

Another theory suggests that hypnic jerks are a vestige of human evolution, remaining from the dawn of mankind when prehistoric humans slept above the ground in high places, safe from predators. In such situations, that **primeval** reflex that is now an annoyance might have been a useful defense against falling, as an individual **haphazardly** drifted to sleep on a tree limb. Sensing the muscles relaxing in a dangerous situation, the brain triggers a hypnic jerk that startles the individual to consciousness for protective purposes. Like other caveman-survival remnants, such as our adrenaline-fueled fight-or-flight response, or irrational fear of snakes and spiders, hypnic jerks could be one of those once necessary responses that has diminished in need but is not disappearing anytime soon.

The good news is that hypnic jerks, however annoying, are not really dangerous; in fact, the reason that there is little conclusive research concerning the phenomenon is because of its harmless nature. Some people have reported falling off of their beds after experiencing a hypnic jerk, but that seems to be the worst case scenario. Remember that the next time you are rudely startled awake just as you were drifting off after a long day, and go back to sleep.

Lesson 14 continued:

33

Choose the most appropriate title for the passage.

A) The Real Origins of the Hypnic Jerk
B) VLPO versus RAS: The Battlefront of the Brain
C) How to Fall Asleep Without Surprises
D) The Mystery of the Hypnic Jerk

34

The purpose of paragraph 4, lines 45-63, is best described as

A) the steps prescribed to alleviate hypnic jerks.
B) an explanation of the brain's control centers of consciousness.
C) a history of the development of the human brain.
D) two hypotheses about the effects of negative emotions on sleep.

35

As it is used in line 57, the word *lethargy* could be used as a synonym for

A) energy.
B) confusion.
C) power.
D) tiredness.

36

Choose the best description of the overall passage.

A) a scholarly essay on the effects of dreams
B) a humorous comparison between scientific facts and anecdotal experience
C) an informative article about a specific element of sleep phenomena
D) an academic report on the diagnosis of sleep disorders

37

Which element of the passage best supports your answer to the previous question?

A) details and explanations of the theories
B) inclusion of abundant data from studies
C) details about several types of sleep disorders
D) theories about how environment affects development

38

The author's attitude toward the study of hypnic jerks is best described as

A) frustrated.
B) unconcerned.
C) enthusiastic.
D) respectful.

39

The best antonym for the word *primeval*, as it is used in line 68, is

A) irritating.
B) modern.
C) perfect.
D) unknown.

40

According to the passage, the most plausible cause of hypnic jerks is

A) on the verge of discovery.
B) a high priority for sleep specialists.
C) not worth mentioning.
D) impossible to say with certainty.

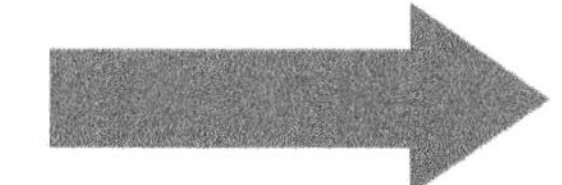

Lesson 14 continued:

41

Choose the line that provides the best evidence for your answer to the previous question.

A) lines 17-20 ("Hypnic jerks…dreams")
B) lines 51-53 ("The first…actions")
C) lines 45-46 ("Although there…jerks")
D) lines 32-35 ("Many dream…mind")

42

Of the possible causes of hypnic jerks, which one is *not* proposed in the passage?

A) negative feelings or concerns
B) a DNA mutation that affects the sleep cycle
C) the brain responding to external noises
D) an ancient, obsolete human reflex

Lesson 14 continued:

Vocabulary: Context Answers

The following sentences contain vocabulary words used in the reading passage. Choose the answer that best completes the sentence. There may be more than one technically correct answer, but one will better exemplify the italicized vocabulary word than the others will.

1) The _____ natural *phenomenon* boggled scientists.
   A. new
   B. inexplicable
   C. obvious
   D. disturbing
   E. strange

2) Ray believed his _____ was predicted by the *ominous* weather.
   A. promotion at work
   B. lunch
   C. good fortune
   D. afternoon nap
   E. bad luck

3) Without meaning to *incite* a fight, Janine accidentally _____ between Joe and Drew.
   A. encouraged the conflict
   B. started a conversation
   C. resolved the dispute
   D. divided her attention
   E. walked

4) The *deterioration* of the abandoned power plant posed a danger to the community because _____.
   A. the workers were careful
   B. there was too much electricity available
   C. the source of power could impact their health
   D. the old storage tanks leaked harmful chemicals
   E. the new apparatus was too efficient

5) It is proven that irregular *deprivation* of food does not aid weight loss; people must eat _____ to lose weight.
   A. moderate amounts
   B. nothing
   C. only sugar
   D. as much as possible
   E. only fatty foods

6) Piper signed up for an *aerobics* class because she heard that _____ would be good for her health.
   A. arts and crafts
   B. heart-strengthening exercise
   C. stretching
   D. weight-lifting
   E. swimming

7) Kim told her doctor that she felt _____ constantly, and he diagnosed her with *lethargy*.
   A. angry
   B. unhappy
   C. hungry
   D. anxious
   E. tired

8) Trent's mother knew that his room was _____, but she was appalled that Paul discarded his clothes so *haphazardly*.
   A. spotless
   B. a little dirty
   C. a disorganized mess
   D. upstairs
   E. dangerous

Lesson 14 continued:

9) Through meditation, the monk claimed the ability to control *autonomic* functions such as _____.
   A. how high he can jump
   B. the rate of his heartbeat
   C. who can see him
   D. his memory
   E. how much he laughs

10) Because the damage was limited to the *cortex* of the kidney, _____.
   A. treatment was impossible
   B. the doctors had no way to access the damage on the inner portion
   C. the whole kidney would have to be removed
   D. surgeons could reach it without making deep incisions
   E. the injury was too deep to repair the kidney

11) The colonists of the island formed the *nucleus* of _____.
   A. the earth
   B. all of history's thought and philosophy
   C. memories of better times in their homeland
   D. a disaster waiting to happen
   E. what would grow into a civilization in the centuries to come

Lesson 14 continued:

Writing Practice

The underlined portion of each sentence provides two pronouns that are often used incorrectly. Choose the pronoun that completes the sentence correctly.

1) The principal was convinced that Helen was the one who / whom had set off the fire alarm.

2) Who / Whom could the veteran mailman be having trouble delivering mail to; why was the address confusing?

3) The odd-looking gentleman said to the group, "I'm looking for Charles, who / whom has expressed interest in becoming an orthodontist."

4) To who / whom do Fred and George owe money?

5) The police detective interrogated the daughter of the man who / whom had evaded the initial sweep of the neighborhood.

6) Who / Whom knows what book claims that the meaning of life is 42?

7) Tilda, who / whom the radio host had asked to substitute for him, prepared for the show.

8) Obi, who / whom was a prominent member of the drama club, appeared quiet and reserved before rehearsal.

9) I can never understand James. Tell me again: He voted that who / whom should be made captain of the football team?

10) Katie, who / whom the judges had not appreciated, spent the entire night streaming sad movies.

11) The general believes that he is the one who / whom monarchs should trust to instruct them in military theory.

12) To who / whom did the teacher explain how to convert Fahrenheit to Celsius?

13) Don't look to see who / whom was responsible; you don't want to know.

14) The movie starred an aspiring actor who / whom a taxi driver had assisted during a traffic jam.

15) The family who / whom finishes the marathon first will win the new car.

Lesson 14 continued:

Vocabulary: Choosing the Right Use

The following sentences contain vocabulary words used in the reading passage. Identify the sentence or sentences that use the italicized vocabulary word properly. We have changed the form of some vocabulary words to provide new contexts; for example, some adjectives and verbs have been used as nouns.

1) A. On the beach, a *phenomenon* of seagulls had flocked and fought over some stray French fries.
   B. "Would you like to work on this project individually, or would you prefer to work in *phenomena*?"
   C. Some people who have lost their arms or legs are still able to feel them—a *phenomenon* called "phantom limb."
   D. To the young boy, who had grown up in the Baja sun, snow was an amazing *phenomenon.*

2) A. As the debate dragged on, it became more and more obvious that neither candidate had an *ominous* opinion of the subject.
   B. The entrance to the abandoned junkyard had an *ominous* notice posted on the front gate that said, "Trespass at Your Own Peril."
   C. Many people who are superstitious consider black cats and smashed mirrors to be *ominous* signs.
   D. "It is not *ominous* whether the park will expand; we have to wait and see how much funding we can get," explained the ranger.

3) A. The president's final powerful statement *incited* loud cheers throughout the rally.
   B. "Would you rather go out for ice cream or for frozen yogurt?" Ramone *incited* to his three children.
   C. In spelling bees, the contestants are allowed to *incite* for only one repetition of the word before they must give an answer.
   D. Nothing *incites* fury in Megan, a passionate animal rights activist, more than the sight of an abused pet.

4) A. Statistics demonstrated *deterioration* in athletic shoe sales, causing investors to avoid shoe manufacturer stock.
   B. As a person ages, he or she will endure a physical and possibly even mental *deterioration.*
   C. When Ginger feels pressured, she notices drastic *deterioration* in stressful dreams in which her teeth fall out.
   D. Over the years, a water leak caused significant *deterioration* of the home's foundation.

5) A. After working double shifts for a week, Heath required a few days to recover from sleep *deprivation.*
   B. *Deprivation* of sunshine can be as damaging to one's health as too much exposure to the sun.
   C. One exciting *deprivation* of Dorinda's new job was that she had two months of vacation time.
   D. Frequent customers of the grocery store received *deprivation*, like coupons and gift certificates.

Lesson 14 continued:

6) A. Due to an injury of her *autonomic* nervous system, Samara has to remind herself to blink occasionally or her eyes become dry and irritated.
   B. Eating too much birthday cake at a party is a common *autonomic* response for most children under the age of ten.
   C. Breathing is an *autonomic* activity and doesn't require any thought—unless, of course, you think about it for a moment.
   D. Mindfulness is an *autonomic* commitment to working to keep one's thoughts in the present moment.

7) A. The question of who would get to sit in the front seat of the car often sparked *lethargy* between Harrison and his brother.
   B. Felice blamed her *lethargy* on the fact that she had been up all night finishing a compelling novel about the Civil War.
   C. My cell phone gives me automatic news updates about the different *lethargy* occurring between foreign countries.
   D. Usually, a big cup of coffee in the morning will prevent, or at least, reduce, my *lethargy* for the day.

8) A. Kindergarteners will often learn about ways to be *primeval*, such as saying "please" and "thank you."
   B. Crying is a *primeval* human behavior; infants instinctively use it to express distress.
   C. Contrary to popular belief, sharks do not actually have a *primeval* desire to kill people; they're simply hungry.
   D. "Please act in a *primeval* manner and push in your chair after you have finished your meal," requested Joni.

9) A. Usually, Maggie got ready in the morning *haphazardly*, but today, having to get to class early, she rushed.
   B. "If you study for the test *haphazardly*, you will likely receive the grade you want," Ms. Lerner said.
   C. The dishes in Nigel's cabinet seemed to be placed *haphazardly*, as though he had put no thought at all into the organization of them.
   D. Mom chose destinations for the road trip *haphazardly* by closing her eyes and sticking pins in a map to indicate stops.

10) A. What function does the *cortex* of the brain serve and just how important is that outer layer?
   B. The *cortex* of Dr. Valance's research is to determine where in the brain mental illness is triggered.
   C. If a person's cerebral *cortex* is damaged, he or she will likely have problems with memory and attention.
   D. The central *cortex* of this workshop will be to train you in woodworking, but we will also do some knitting projects," said Lisa.

Lesson 14 continued:

11) A. The *reticular* arrangement of the region's communication lines ensured that information would be transmitted even if small portions of the grid failed.
    B. Under a microscope, one can observe the *reticular* structure of a leaf's many interconnected veins supplying nutrients to all the cells.
    C. "Only a true genius could solve such an incredibly *reticular* math problem," said Brenner about the complicated numbers before him.
    D. The directions Stan provided us for how to get to the bowling alley were so *reticular* that we had him repeat them four times.

Lesson 14 continued:

Synonyms and Antonyms

Match the word with its *antonym*.

1) incite	**A.** energy
2) haphazardly	**B.** improvement
3) lethargy	**C.** discourage
4) deprivation	**D.** gain
5) deterioration	**E.** carefully

Match the word with its *synonym*.

6) ominous	**A.** protection
7) aerobics	**B.** automatic
8) cortex	**C.** exercise
9) autonomic	**D.** menacing
10) phenomenon	**E.** center
11) nucleus	**F.** rarity

END
of
LESSON 14

Lesson 15

Questions 43–52 are based on the following passages.

The authors of the following two passages take different approaches to discuss an ancient threat to humanity.

Passage 1

Yersinia pestis is a bacterium that causes flu-like symptoms, swollen, painful lymph nodes, and, in its most severe form, pneumonia, respiratory failure, eruption of pus-filled glands, and a blackening and **gangrene** (decomposition and death) of skin and other tissues, especially on fingers, toes, and noses. The plague is most noted for its causing the Black Death, a 14th-century **pandemic** that killed an estimated 75 to 200 million people, or two-fifths of the world's population. *Pestis*, however, didn't begin as a killer; the bacteria that cause plague once posed only a threat of gastrointestinal infection. It was a small change, somewhere in the strain's history, that transformed it from a nuisance into a lethal **menace**.

Scientists attribute the bacterium's enhanced lethality to the random mutation of a gene for a surface protein, called a plasminogen activator, or Pla. Research has traced the ancestry of *Yersinia pestis* back to a relatively harmless stomach pathogen called *Y. pseudotuberculosis*, which causes only mild diarrhea. The intrusion and **subsequent** mutation of Pla produced different, quickly evolving strains of the disease, among them the strains that cause bubonic plague, septicemic plague, and pneumonic plague. The bubonic plague strain of *Y. pestis* travels via lymphatic vessels to a lymph node, which swells and causes the host to experience flu-like symptoms. The strain that causes the septicemic plague is the rarest form of *Y. pestis*, occurring when bacteria enter the bloodstream. The strain for **pneumonic** plague attacks the lungs. It spreads to the respiratory system from the bloodstream, and it is the only strain that can be spread from person to person without an outside **vector**, or transmitter; the transmission can happen through inhaling **aerosolized** plague bacteria.

Y. pestis is a mutant variety, hindered by an inability to survive outside its host, which means it cannot directly infiltrate host cells. To ensure its own **propagation**, the strain disables its host's immune system by injecting toxins into defense cells, such as **macrophages**, which are responsible for detecting infections. Macrophages protect the body from foreign particles through a process called phagocytosis, during which they engulf foreign particles and trap them in an internal cavity called a phagosome. When a macrophage phagocytoses *Y. pestis*, the bacteria continue to multiply inside the macrophage and, once delivered to the host's lymphatic system, kill the macrophage and escape. With the defense cells compromised, and a new resistance to attack that it develops while in the host macrophages, *Y. pestis* reproduces **unimpeded**, causing the host to become ill. Interestingly, people who survive the bubonic plague have been shown to also be resistant to HIV, the virus that causes Acquired Immune Deficiency Syndrome (AIDS), probably owing to the similar way in which the two diseases spread.

The most common vector of *Y. pestis* is the flea, and the most dangerous variant is a particular species of flea called *Xenopsylla cheopis*, more informally referred to as the Oriental rat flea. Oriental rat fleas tend to feed on rats and other rodents that carry plague. They also possess a physical characteristic that increases the likelihood of transmission. Plague bacteria block the digestive tract of the rat flea. When feeding, a plague-bearing flea regurgitates its plague-infested blood meal back into the host, infecting it.

Typically, in response to a flea bite, human tissue forms a blood clot, which prevents bleeding, allows the wound to heal, and traps harmful bacteria in the clot, preventing its spread. *Y. pestis* with Pla disrupts the body's ability to contain bacteria at the sites of infection. Pla prompts the breakdown of an important clotting protein called fibrin, causing clots to dissolve and bacteria to multiply unimpeded.

Lesson 15 continued:

Passage 2

Bubonic plague, black plague, or black death, whichever term is applied, is a horrifying, disfiguring disease caused by bites from an infected flea. If untreated, a localized swelling quickly leads to intense fever, then chills, followed by seizures and the **eponymous** symptom that gives the condition its nickname—the general blackening of body parts as tissue dies. As gangrene sets in, the skin decomposes, causing extreme pain. Death used to be the inevitable result, but modern medicine can treat the disease easily if caught early. The history of the plague is a long and fascinating one—one that changed the course of history numerous times.

Traveling by land along Central Asia's Silk Road and by sea via European ships, the plague inspired an ugly chapter in human history. From 1346 to 1353, the disease caused societal abandonment, **scapegoating**, self-mutilation, and looting, not to mention the death of 30-60% of Europe's total population and 100 million people worldwide.

It is misleading to describe the bubonic plague as just a "chapter" in history. For one thing, the populations affected didn't reach their pre-plague levels until the 17th century, partially due to reoccurrences of the plague. Furthermore, research shows that bubonic plague goes much further back than previously thought and is anything but extinct.

In 2015 alone, the US Centers for Disease Control and Prevention identified fifteen cases of bubonic plague in the United States, four of which proved fatal. This figure is up from the national average of seven cases annually, although the rate is lower than in 2006, which topped out at seventeen.

The disease usually occurs between late spring and early fall and is most often found in the semi-rural western US, particularly in New Mexico, Arizona, and Colorado, although the aforementioned fifteen cases occurred in eight states, owing to travel.

Luckily, with expeditious diagnosis and treatment, survival rates are as high as 84%. Delaying or omitting treatment, however, increases mortality rates to 93%. In addition to getting medical care upon the development of symptoms, precautions against plague include wearing long pants, using insect repellant, treating pets for fleas, and removing food sources and nesting areas for neighborhood rodent populations, such as open trash cans and brushy woodlines, as the disease's strain, *Yersinia pestis*, is still usually transmitted through rats and fleas.

There are multiple historical outbreaks of the bubonic strain besides the notorious **medieval** example, including the Plague of Justinian in Constantinople in the 6th century and the Third Pandemic in China in the 1850s. It had even been suspected as the primary agent in the Antonine Plague in the 2nd century and the Plague of Athens 2,500 years ago, both considered **catalysts** to Rome's and Greece's separate declines. Without molecular evidence from skeletal material, however, the theory remains inconclusive.

To determine what caused the extensive spread of Black Death, the Center for GeoGenetics at the University of Copenhagen examined DNA tooth samples of Bronze Age individuals from both Europe and Asia and found evidence of plague infection 4,800 years ago. The University of Gothenburg in Sweden went back further, examining 101 individuals by collecting 89 billion raw DNA samples. It found seven individuals affected by the strain, establishing evidence that the plague struck 5,783 years ago.

Given the plague's devastating effects in the 14th century, how did earlier populations survive? It seems that there should be more recorded incidents of **catastrophic** plague outbreaks. Can the blame fall on the plague's ability to spread with new trade routes, or are there other factors?

There are, in fact, differences between Bronze Age and Iron Age samples of plague. The first is the earlier presence of a **flagellum**, a cell appendage like a tail used primarily for movement. The tail allowed the bacteria more mobility, but importantly, it rendered them more recognizable to human immune systems, allowing them to quickly identify the bacteria and **stave** off infection. When the bacteria with this flagellum were rapidly killed off, bacteria without it reproduced at a greater rate, resulting in a strain more difficult for the immune system to identify. When the new strain further developed a mutant toxin, its ability to kill became much more **formidable**. Using scientific dating methods, this change is estimated to have taken roughly 1,000 years to develop, and took place at roughly 1,000 BCE—just in time for the infamous Plague of Athens. Modern scientists, however, believe that the Athens epidemic

Lesson 15 continued:

may not actually have been the result of true bubonic plague, but, instead, deadly combinations of smallpox, typhus, and hemorrhagic fever.

Unlike prehistoric or medieval plague victims, modern society is not generally inclined to believe that bubonic plague was divine **retribution**. It is a disease like any other, but quite unlike any other in its effects on humanity. The world's population is currently over seven billion. Cancer kills more than eight million people each year. Heart disease kills seven million. Stroke kills six million. A plague pandemic equal to the black death would kill upwards of two billion people. It would be wise to stay well ahead of such a devastating bug because it is the type that changes the world.

43

According to the explanation provided in Passage 1, lines 36-52, once inside a host, the plague bacteria can be said to

A) create protein sanctuaries before entering a dormant state.
B) defend against phagosomes by mutating.
C) imitate immune cells and become carriers for HIV.
D) use macrophages as vehicles for safe transport.

44

Choose the lines that provide the best evidence for your answer to the previous question.

A) lines 36-38 ("*Y. pestis*...cells")
B) lines 45-48 ("When a...escape")
C) lines 52-53 ("people who...HIV")
D) lines 48-50 ("With the...macrophages")

45

As used in Passage 1, line 39, *propagation* is most similar to

A) excess.
B) division.
C) scarcity.
D) reproduction.

46

The purpose of Passage 1, paragraph 2 (lines 15-35), is best described as

A) a continuation of the description of plague's high mortality rate.
B) a synopsis of the evolution and strains of *Y. pestis.*
C) a transition to an explanation of plague's effect on fleas.
D) a counterargument to the author's claim about plague's random mutation.

47

Choose the possible title that accurately describes the content of both passages.

A) Common Vectors of Plague Bacteria
B) *Yersinia pestis*
C) History of the Bubonic Plague
D) The Value of Microphages

Lesson 15 continued:

48

Choose the statement that most accurately contrasts the style of the passages.

A) Passage 1 is formal and scholarly, while Passage 2 is subjective and informal.
B) Passage 1 shows bias for modern methods of detection, while Passage 2 supports unproven methods.
C) Passage 1 is written for a general, academic audience, while Passage 2 is intended specifically for microbiologists.
D) Passage 1 provides more details about historic events than Passage 2 does.

49

The authors of both passages would definitely agree with which one of the following statements?

A) Brushy woodlines are a genuine threat to world health.
B) Plague was once completely harmless to people.
C) Plague mutated at some point in history.
D) Pneumonic plague is spread mostly through rat fleas.

50

As it is used in Passage 2, line 39, *expeditious* most nearly means

A) substantial.
B) thoughtful.
C) immediate.
D) prudent.

51

Which statement best describes why the following quotation from Passage 2 is inherently contradictory to the overall passage?

> A plague pandemic equal to the black death would kill upwards of two billion people. It would be wise to stay well ahead of such a devastating bug because it is the type that changes the world.

A) Modern treatment greatly reduces the mortality rate of bubonic plague.
B) The historic pandemics occurred without warning.
C) There is no known way to defeat the bacteria that cause plague.
D) The author establishes the deadly nature of *Y. pestis*.

52

Choose the line from Passage 2 that provides the best evidence to support your answer to the previous question.

A) lines 28-30 ("In 2015…fatal")
B) lines 25-27 ("Furthermore, research…extinct")
C) lines 16-20 ("From 1346…worldwide")
D) lines 9-11 ("Death used…early")

Lesson 15 continued:

Vocabulary: Context Answers

The following sentences contain vocabulary words used in the reading passages. Choose the answer that best completes the sentence. There may be more than one technically correct answer, but one will better exemplify the italicized vocabulary word than the others will.

1) The disease originated in America before becoming *pandemic*; it can now _____.
   A. infect animals
   B. be easily contained
   C. be found in China
   D. spread through the air
   E. kill those who are infected

2) The squirrels in the attic became a *menace*, rather than an annoyance, when they _____.
   A. slept quietly during the day
   B. started biting people
   C. left the attic for good
   D. stayed for more than a month
   E. could not be exterminated

3) All of the events _____ Leonard's demotion were crystal clear, but everything *subsequent* was a blur until the day that he was fired.
   A. surrounding
   B. after
   C. causing
   D. leading up to
   E. caused by

4) Biologists did not expect housecats to become a *vector* for the fatal bacteria and are _____.
   A. worried that the housecats might die
   B. upset that their pets are ill
   C. glad to have found a cure
   D. surprised that they do not show symptoms
   E. concerned that cats could transmit the bacteria to humans

5) The scientists accelerated the *propagation* of the organisms so that _____.
   A. they would have enough to conduct their experiment
   B. the microbes could be exterminated more quickly
   C. they would become more contagious
   D. the danger of exposure would be reduced
   E. they would need fewer nutrients

6) The Thompson family expected to be _____ pay the parking fee, so they were surprised when they could enter the garage *unimpeded.*
   A. exempt from having to
   B. praised for always remembering to
   C. reprimanded for forgetting to
   D. arrested so that they would
   E. stopped at the gate to

Lesson 15 continued:

7) Because of Ingrid's _____, the doctors knew that her infection was primarily *pneumonic*.
   A. sneezing
   B. coughing
   C. stomach cramps
   D. nausea
   E. headache

8) Wade preferred *aerosolized* sunscreen because _____.
   A. it could be sprayed on in thin coats
   B. the thick cream was very protective
   C. it was better than gel sunscreen
   D. the spray was sticky
   E. he could use it as lotion as well

9) Doctors were concerned about Paula's _____ because her *macrophages* were diminishing in number.
   A. digestion
   B. respiratory system
   C. mental health
   D. nervous system
   E. immune system

10) William Penn, the *eponymous* proprietor of _____, was a Quaker.
   A. Virginia
   B. Delaware
   C. Maryland
   D. Pennsylvania
   E. Philadelphia

11) Dr. Mendez needed to determine the *catalysts* of the ecological collapse to discover its _____.
   A. effects
   B. process
   C. cause
   D. uses
   E. history

12) The hurricane proved to be *catastrophic*; because of the storm, several trees _____.
   A. were more fruitful in the autumn
   B. fell on houses, killing the residents
   C. began to rot from too much water
   D. diverted lightning away from houses
   E. lost all of their leaves

13) If he failed to *stave* off the flu that had already infected his siblings, Reggie would _____.
   A. surely miss the concert on Friday
   B. be better in a few hours
   C. probably not contract the flu
   D. get a flu shot
   E. be the only person in his house who was not sick

14) The other wrestler, Daniel, was such a *formidable* opponent that Dale feared Daniel might _____ the match.
   A. be hurt in
   B. lose
   C. injure him in
   D. forfeit
   E. tie

Lesson 15 continued:

15) Yasmin feared *retribution* for _____.
   A. walking to school
   B. eating the last popsicle
   C. giving her brother the perfect gift
   D. doing her homework carefully
   E. drenching her brother with water

16) During the Civil War, long before the discovery of antibiotics, many soldiers _____ due to *gangrene*.
   A. felt ill
   B. were sent home
   C. lost limbs
   D. switched sides
   E. survived

17) Even though the entire group had cheated, *scapegoating* Ron _____.
   A. earned them an A
   B. diverted the blame away from the other students
   C. was necessary
   D. meant that they would fail
   E. got everyone else in trouble

18) The *medieval* painting was created in _____.
   A. central Europe
   B. the Middle Ages
   C. 1900
   D. Central America
   E. Madrid

19) Without *flagellum*, microorganisms _____.
   A. cannot eat larger particles
   B. will die
   C. cannot easily transport themselves
   D. reproduce quickly
   E. photosynthesize for energy

Lesson 15 continued:

Writing Practice

The underlined portion of each sentence possibly contains a flaw related to the construction of the sentence. Select the answer that best corrects the flaw. Select NO CHANGE if the underlined portion is correct.

1) Wear your seatbelt, remembering to signal when you turn, and avoiding the curb are three crucial components of a driving test.
   A. NO CHANGE
   B. Your seatbelt
   C. To wear your seatbelt
   D. Wearing your seatbelt

2) The job applicant's résumé outlined her many strengths: She was organized, leadership, and dedication.
   A. NO CHANGE
   B. she could organize
   C. organization
   D. organized

3) "Unfortunately, wanting something and when you receive it do not always go hand-in-hand," lamented my father.
   A. NO CHANGE
   B. receiving
   C. to receive
   D. the reception of

4) Surprisingly, the jackets sold at Clothes Galore were more expensive than other stores.
   A. NO CHANGE
   B. buying from other stores
   C. those sold at other stores
   D. the prices at other stores

5) Rock music, a folk singer, and classical music were just a few of the musical categories represented at the showcase.
   A. NO CHANGE
   B. folk
   C. folk music
   D. the folk genre

Lesson 15 continued:

6) Broadway shows were practically Eleanor's religion; she passionately believed in and stood by her favorite productions.
   A. NO CHANGE
   B. believed and stood by
   C. believed and stood, in and by,
   D. both believed and stood by

7) Berke wears sandals in the summer, boots in the winter, and sneakers are worn by him in the spring.
   A. NO CHANGE
   B. and in the spring, he wears sneakers.
   C. and sneakers in the spring.
   D. and in the spring, sneakers.

8) Whether in spring, in autumn, or winter, the university's campus was absolutely beautiful.
   A. NO CHANGE
   B. also the winter
   C. during winter
   D. in winter

9) My mom firmly believes that it is easier writing a letter than to send an email, which is obviously not true.
   A. NO CHANGE
   B. to write a letter
   C. for a letter to be written
   D. that I write a letter

10) The vice principal's speech at graduation emphasized that our class had the capacity to make a difference in the world and that using our creativity would help us in all of our future endeavors.
   A. NO CHANGE
   B. using our creativity
   C. to use our creativity
   D. the creativity used

Lesson 15 continued:

Vocabulary: Choosing the Right Use

The following sentences contain vocabulary words used in the reading passages. Identify the sentence or sentences that use the italicized vocabulary word properly. We have changed the form of some vocabulary words to provide new contexts; for example, some adjectives and verbs have been used as nouns.

1) A. Texting is a *pandemic* among the world population that has truly revolutionized communication.
   B. A flu *pandemic* across the college campus forced the school to close down for a week.
   C. Luckily, scientists were able to quarantine the infected citizens before the disease became a *pandemic*.
   D. Modern *pandemics* are vastly different from those of other decades; I would never wear my hair in a style from the 1980s.

2) A. Mosquito hawks look like *menaces* but are actually harmless and even eat mosquitos.
   B. The author used so many *menaces* to depict her scenery that the description of a single flower was three pages long.
   C. Jamie thought that the large bear would be a *menace*, but it sauntered by without paying any attention to her.
   D. Detective Franklin scanned every last *menace* of the crime scene for a clue as to how the victim had been killed.

3) A. The horror movie received a PG-13 rating because children might consider the monsters *subsequent*.
   B. The downpour and *subsequent* rainbow reminded me why spring is my favorite season.
   C. The cat, who found the thunder to be *subsequent*, hid under the couch until the storm was over.
   D. In light of the condemning evidence against Morton, the public expected a conviction *subsequent* to his arrest.

4) A. Half of the room agreed with Mr. Rein's *propagation*, but the other half seemed wary of his idea.
   B. "I hereby approved the Plant Alliance's *propagation* of having an annual citywide gardening day," said the mayor.
   C. Quick *propagation* of the news was due largely to everyone's easy access to the Internet.
   D. To prevent the *propagation* of strep throat through the whole family, my mom had me stay in my room while I was still contagious.

Lesson 15 continued:

5) A. After the security guards removed Kate's protesting former boyfriend from the church, her wedding continued *unimpeded.*
B. "Please stop that loud tapping noise," snapped Monica, *unimpeded* by the sound.
C. The professor could not proceed with his lecture *unimpeded*; students were constantly interrupting him with questions.
D. Jake seemed *unimpeded* by the rock concert, at which the rest of his friends were having quite an enjoyable time.

6) A. In the midst of the murder mystery, the media *scapegoated* Randy, who was the last person to have been seen with the victim.
B. The school's administration decided to *scapegoat* Sally as Student of the Year, which included a cash prize of $100.
C. "Do you remember which novels were *scapegoated* as *New York Times* bestsellers last year?" asked Missy.
D. The siblings knew who had broken Mom's antique clock, but they chose to *scapegoat* Gina, the youngest in the family, because she couldn't yet form the words to deny it.

7) A. "Should we update the textbook so that the information in it is not *medieval*?" asked the editor.
B. If the path were not so *medieval*, riddled with ditches and thorns, I would take it.
C. The *medieval* suits of armor were the most popular attraction at the museum.
D. The carnival ride seemed *medieval*, but Charlotte assured me that it had been around for a long time.

8) A. Nuclear power plants often keep waste products from reactions in a self-contained *catalyst.*
B. The *catalyst* held a combination of chemicals that Dr. Fredriks argued could be the key to repairing the ozone layer.
C. The reaction between the two chemical compounds will not begin until a *catalyst* is added to the mix.
D. Chandra's comment about makeup products acted as a *catalyst* to a discussion of animal cruelty.

9) A. Had the town not been warned of the tornado ahead of time, I imagine the effects would have been even more *catastrophic*.
B. Professor Klapman looked around at the *catastrophic* results of the experiment—shattered glassware, scorched walls, and a small fire on the lab counter.
C. The *catastrophic* fireworks were gorgeous, although they frightened every dog in the neighborhood.
D. The grand prismatic canyon at Yellowstone Park has *catastrophic*, unbelievable views.

Lesson 15 continued:

10) A. A hyperactive child, Daniella could be *staved* off only by the sound of her mother singing a classic lullaby.
    B. Wearing a seatbelt is one way to *stave* off serious injury in the event of a motor vehicle accident.
    C. "Hopefully, the storm will *stave* off soon so that we can get to Morgan's beach house this weekend," Preston said.
    D. "I read somewhere that eating fruit *staves* off scurvy," said Bo.

11) A. Jaclyn found it much easier to run *formidable* races than long-lasting ones.
    B. The waves appeared especially *formidable* today, so novice surfers chose to opt out.
    C. Though the football player's size was certainly *formidable*, his opponent could run faster and defend himself better.
    D. Morris disliked driving; the more *formidable* the route, the more likely he was to agree to take us there.

12) A. As *retribution* for my breaking his lawnmower, Corey stole mine in the middle of the night.
    B. "If I may offer my *retribution*," said Gwen, "I think we should delegate tasks based on each team member's greatest strength."
    C. Melany brought homemade brownies, cookies, and cupcakes as her *retribution* to the annual bake sale.
    D. The employee who alerted the media to his company's criminal behavior expected *retribution* in the form of termination.

13) A. Luckily, the *gangrene* of cells turned out to be benign, not cancerous, as the doctors had suspected.
    B. *Gangrene* followed in the days after her severe frostbite, rendering Lil's feet useless.
    C. The Native Americans knew that certain herbs applied to open wounds seemed to reduce the risk of *gangrene*.
    D. The *gangrene* of bug bites that had accumulated on my knee became unbearably itchy.

14) A. As a lung specialist, Dr. Gasp possessed a great deal of *pneumonic* knowledge, which he used to help his patients.
    B. "Do you happen to know any *pneumonic* devices I could use to remember the order of the planets?" asked Marjorie.
    C. The *pneumonic* wind on the mountain made us feel even colder.
    D. Amanda's *pneumonic* infection caused her to have difficulty breathing for a few days.

15) A. Amy prefers *aerosolized* paint because it is typically easier to apply.
    B. Left in the sun, the child's clay became *aerosolized* and unable to be reformed.
    C. Chase rattled his *aerosolized* deodorant can before spraying some on himself.
    D. *Aerosolized* by a kiln, Abigail's pottery was ready to be given to her dad as a Father's Day present.

Lesson 15 continued:

16) A. "The *macrophages* are essentially the security guards of the human body," explained Dr. No.
    B. New York City is home to many tall *macrophages* that gleam in the daylight and light up at night.
    C. My father is a construction worker and assists his team in building extraordinary *macrophages.*
    D. An individual becomes ill when his or her *macrophages* are unable to fight off infection.

17) A. The poet enjoyed using *eponymous* pairs—night and day, black and white, etc.—in his works.
    B. Jerry Seinfeld's fame as a comedian led to the creation of an *eponymous* television series in which he played the leading role.
    C. "Are you so vain that you would seriously name all your children after yourself?" I asked Maureen about the *eponymous* names.
    D. "Sneaking out at night is *eponymous* compared to how we have raised you," scolded Dad.

18) A. The scientist examined two protozoa side-by-side to see which one had the longest *flagellum.*
    B. "When you dive, the position of your arms and *flagella* is vital to your safety," explained Coach Bill.
    C. Did you know that the presence of a *flagellum* aids microscopic organisms in swimming?
    D. Mia decided to exercise her *flagella* today, spending extra time on the leg-lift machine at the gym.

19) A. Be careful not to be bitten by a tick, as it is likely a *vector* of Lyme disease or Rocky Mountain spotted fever.
    B. After retracing the lice outbreak in the school, the nurse discovered that the *vector* had been a single third-grader.
    C. Sammy's *vector* to build a boat made out of cardboard required several of his friends to help him out.
    D. Dad sent all the siblings an elaborate email that included every detail of his *vector* for our family vacation.

Lesson 15 continued:

Synonyms and Antonyms

Match the word with its *antonym*.

1) unimpeded	**A.** solidified
2) pandemic	**B.** deterred
3) aerosolized	**C.** preceding
4) subsequent	**D.** isolated
5) formidable	**E.** allow
6) eponymous	**F.** blockage
7) catalyst	**G.** harmless
8) stave	**H.** anonymous
9) retribution	**I.** forgiveness

Lesson 15 continued:

Synonyms and Antonyms

Match the word with its *synonym*.

1)	vector	**A.**	danger
2)	menace	**B.**	reproduction
3)	propagation	**C.**	carrier
4)	pneumonic	**D.**	respiratory
5)	medieval	**E.**	decay
6)	gangrene	**F.**	blame
7)	scapegoat	**G.**	disastrous
8)	flagellum	**H.**	old-fashioned
9)	catastrophic	**I.**	whip

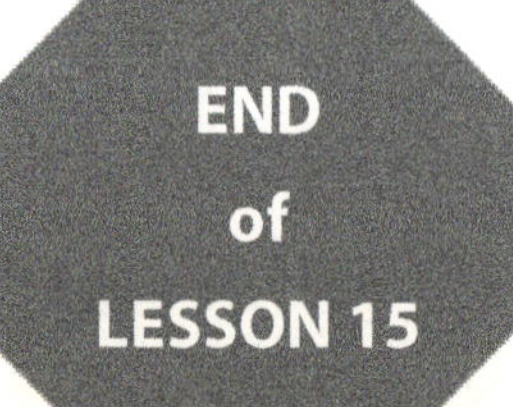

Lesson 16

Writing and Language Test

A set of questions accompanies each passage. The questions will ask you to make editorial decisions that improve or correct language, grammar, and construction errors in the paragraphs, including any accompanying graphics. Read the passage and then choose the best answer to each of the questions. In some instances, no change will be necessary.

Questions 1–11 are based on the following passage.

— 1 —

Typically, when someone says "White House," the first person who comes to mind is the president of the United States; the truth is, however, that the White House is less the home of the president and more a complicated machine consisting of many moving parts, big and small, with some you never knew existed. Consider, for example, the Graphics and Calligraphy Office.

— 2 —

[1] Long performed by Romans, Chinese, and Greeks, **{ 1 }** calligraphy, the art of creating decorative lettering, is relevant beyond the making of fancy wedding invitations and college diplomas. [2] In the East Wing of the White House as a unit of the Social Office, the Calligraphy Office **{ 2 }** Staff Members are responsible for the preparation of invitations, place cards, awards, and other official documents on behalf of the president. [3] Many of the *hands* in use, or specific calligraphy styles, have been employed for many administrations. **{ 3 }**

— 3 —

The world-class calligraphers work under carefully constructed conditions to create the elegant hands. Their desks are angled in such a way as to achieve the maximum level of steadiness and comfort. The office itself is spacious and full of natural light so that calligraphers can easily distinguish between ink colors, as **fluorescent** light can distort appearances.

1

A) NO CHANGE
B) calligraphy the art of creating decorative lettering
C) calligraphy the art, of creating, decorative lettering,
D) calligraphy the art of creating decorative lettering,

2

A) NO CHANGE
B) staff members
C) Staff members
D) staff Members

3

Choose the most logical place for the writer to insert the following sentence:

> One hand used for dinner invitations, for example, has roots from as far back as the John Adams administration.

A) before sentence [1]
B) after sentence [1]
C) after sentence [2]
D) after sentence [3]

Lesson 16 continued:

— 4 —

{ 4 } Having the job of presidential calligrapher is not a cushy job by any means. The profession demands a degree of concentration and attention that only a balance of discipline and talent can provide. In a calligrapher's world, every tiny stroke of a pen or a brush counts. Furthermore, the modern age of information and global commitment has brought with it tight deadlines and additional responsibilities. In 2006, the White House calligraphers crafted approximately 19,000 individual invitations for holiday dinners and receptions, expertly—or insanely—hand-lettering each one. Projects that decades ago allowed several weeks for completion now might receive a few hours of notice. For an especially busy, important evening, such as the state dinner, calligraphers remain on standby in case of a crisis related to their responsibilities, such as a last-minute VIP who needs a place card. They are, for all { 5 } intensive purposes, an emergency hand-written note squad.

— 5 —

Though most calligraphy projects are { 6 } hand-done manually, with pen and ink, modern technology alleviates a few of the **nuances** involved in the process, helping tremendously with the tight deadlines of a world larger than one in which pen and ink were the only available tools. In the past, a single misspelling or botch would force the calligrapher to start a project from { 7 } scratch. Now, computers can be used to make some of the fixes. Handwritten pieces can be scanned into a computer and digitally **manipulated** or duplicated. This **contemporary** technique might seem like cheating for the country's official calligraphy office, but it actually requires a great deal of expertise. Calligraphers use software and their discerning eyes for spacing and layout to render custom **typefaces** and **fonts** even on digital documents, bringing **exclusivity** and class to their work even when demand forces them to work in the digital realm.

4

A) NO CHANGE
B) The presidential calligrapher
C) Presidential calligrapher
D) Working as the presidential calligrapher

5

A) NO CHANGE
B) intents and purposes
C) intended purposes
D) intends and purposes

6

A) NO CHANGE
B) drawn
C) done in hand
D) done manually

7

Choose the answer that best combines the sentences at the underlined portion.

A) scratch—now: computers
B) scratch, now, computers
C) scratch; now, computers
D) scratch: Now computers

Lesson 16 continued:

— 6 —

{ **8** } <u>Many citizens find the idea of presidential, in-house calligraphers to be rather **superfluous**.</u> There are at least three of them on the White House's payroll, with each making **salaries** close to { **9** } <u>$100,000 dollars</u> a year—a sum that occasionally arises as a point of political contention, depending on who is in office and who is complaining (see chart). Frustration concerning the high salaries of these workers came to a head in 2014, when the White House temporarily closed its doors to the public, **curtailing** public tours because of budget cuts, while continuing to pay a **substantial** sum of money for fancy invitations. { **10** } <u>Irregardless</u>, people who heard the general details of this situation became confused and even outraged. In this instance, the historical value of the centuries-old tradition and the inherent class and quality it brings to the office of the president of the most powerful nation on Earth, seems to have won. { **11** }

White House Employee Annual Salaries (2015)

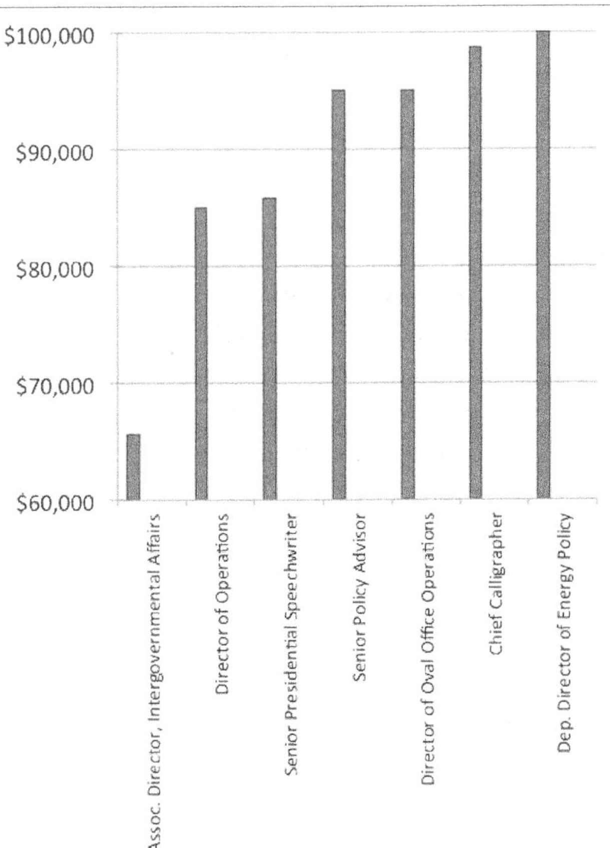

8

A) NO CHANGE
B) Many citizens regard the presidential calligrapher positions as superfluous.
C) Many citizens find the idea of calligraphers to be superfluous.
D) Many citizens, on the idea of in-house, presidential calligraphers, find the idea superfluous.

9

A) NO CHANGE
B) $100,000
C) $100 thousand
D) $1 hundred thousand

10

A) NO CHANGE
B) Regardless
C) Justifiably
D) However

11

The chart has a weak connection to the passage. The best way to incorporate the data into the passage would be to

A) provide the specific dollar amount of the calligrapher's salary.
B) explain the increase in wages due to inflation.
C) analyze the job duties of the Senior Presidential Speechwriter.
D) discuss the salary and duties of Chief Calligrapher as compared to other official positions.

Lesson 16 continued:

Vocabulary: Context Answers

The following sentences contain vocabulary words used in the reading passage. Choose the answer that best completes the sentence. There may be more than one technically correct answer, but one will better exemplify the italicized vocabulary word than the others will.

1) Turning on the *fluorescent* _____ the kitchen.
   A. vacuum proved effective in cleaning
   B. air conditioner kept the family cool in
   C. overhead light helped me find the pan in
   D. music caused my sister to sing and dance in
   E. furnace enabled us to successfully heat

2) A master chef has trained his or her palate to differentiate *nuances* _____.
   A. of bold, overpowering flavors
   B. everyone notices in a dish
   C. that can easily overwhelm the senses with a single taste
   D. found in common recipes
   E. that are undetectable to amateurs

3) The graphic artist used _____ to *manipulate* this month's magazine cover.
   A. a photo editing program
   B. a word processor
   C. a camera
   D. an advertisement
   E. creativity

4) Sally likes to read *contemporary* books _____.
   A. from her great-grandmother's library
   B. about the latest trends in technology
   C. by scientists, psychologists, and philosophers
   D. meant to inspire her imagination
   E. without any illustrations

5) Because _____, the designer chose a simple, bold *typeface* for the billboard advertisement.
   A. drivers needed to be able to read the text while passing by at high speed
   B. the last artist had been fired
   C. the customer likes elaborate, fancy writing
   D. Because of the size of the project and the added expenses of artwork
   E. the look of the words was secondary to the picture of the product

6) The *font* of the _____ for emphasis.
   A. speaker increased in volume
   B. sentence included an exclamation point
   C. gavel's pounding meant to be
   D. word *severe* was italicized
   E. audience cleared their throats

Lesson 16 continued:

7) Mara's _____ demonstrated her party's *exclusivity*.
   A. choice of music
   B. last-minute cancellation
   C. lack of guests
   D. friendly attitude
   E. rule of "invite-only"

8) The many necklaces _____ *superfluous*.
   A. displayed in the store looked affordable and
   B. in the museum were stolen by someone
   C. around Naomi's neck seemed
   D. that Greg made by hand were
   E. at the thrift shop were old but

9) Jordan's recent increase in *salary* gave him the _____.
   A. freedom to live without worrying about bills
   B. motivation to go to the doctor
   C. courage to try new things
   D. burden of working more hours
   E. last clue he needed to solve the crime

10) When _____ the principal had to *curtail* art classes.
   A. students complained about having no creative outlet,
   B. school was closed for a day because of bad weather,
   C. a parent asked, "Why are you offering Painting and Drawing?"
   D. the school board could not find a substitute for the art teacher,
   E. one student complained about the art teacher's disciplinary methods,

11) Investors were not interested in funding the new business unless there would be a *substantial* _____.
   A. cocktail party for those involved
   B. week designated to run background checks on the owner
   C. dependence on capable contractors
   D. program instituted that defined the owner's expectations
   E. return on their money

Lesson 16 continued:

Writing Practice

Each of the following sentences contains a modifying phrase that may or may not be clear or correct. Choose the answer that best corrects the sentence while retaining the intended meaning of the original sentence. Select NO CHANGE if the provided sentence is correct.

1) The clerk sold the skirt to the woman with the leopard print.
   A. NO CHANGE
   B. With the leopard print, the clerk sold the skirt to the woman.
   C. The clerk with the leopard print sold the skirt to the woman.
   D. The clerk sold the skirt with the leopard print to the woman.

2) During the snowstorm, Declan went outside and found a dog in his coat.
   A. NO CHANGE
   B. Declan went outside during the snowstorm and found a dog in his coat.
   C. During the snowstorm, Declan went outside in his coat and found a dog.
   D. During the snowstorm and wearing his coat, Declan went outside and found a dog.

3) Over the radio, two cars were reported stolen by the police last week.
   A. NO CHANGE
   B. Last week, over the radio, two cars were reported stolen by the police.
   C. Last week, the police reported over the radio that two cars had been stolen.
   D. The police reported two cars stolen over the radio last week.

4) When we reached the top of the mountain, we were awed by the stunning view.
   A. NO CHANGE
   B. We were awed by the stunning view climbing to the top of the mountain.
   C. We climbed, awed by the stunning view, to the top of the mountain.
   D. Climbing to the top of the mountain, the stunning view awed us.

5) The fussy toddler only wants to eat macaroni and cheese.
   A. NO CHANGE
   B. Macaroni and cheese is only the food the fussy toddler wants to eat.
   C. The fussy toddler wants to eat only macaroni and cheese.
   D. The only fussy toddler wants to eat macaroni and cheese.

6) An avid birdwatcher, Judy studied the bald eagle using binoculars in the tree.
   A. NO CHANGE
   B. An avid birdwatcher, Judy used binoculars to study the bald eagle in the tree.
   C. Judy, an avid birdwatcher, studied the bald eagle in the tree using binoculars.
   D. An avid birdwatcher, Judy studied the bald eagle in the tree using binoculars.

Lesson 16 continued:

7) Gabriel barely hit the baseball thirty feet.
   A. NO CHANGE
   B. Barely, Gabriel hit the baseball thirty feet.
   C. Gabriel hit the baseball barely thirty feet.
   D. Gabriel hit the baseball thirty feet barely.

8) Michelle served cookies to her guests on fine china.
   A. NO CHANGE
   B. Michelle served on fine china cookies to her guests.
   C. To her guests, on fine china, Michelle served cookies.
   D. Michelle served cookies on fine china to her guests.

9) Uncle Pete heard there was a riot on the evening news.
   A. NO CHANGE
   B. While on the evening news, Uncle Pete heard there was a riot.
   C. Uncle Pete, on the evening news, heard there was a riot.
   D. While listening to the evening news, Uncle Pete heard there was a riot.

10) We had plenty of time before takeoff, so we ate the meal we had bought at the airport slowly.
   A. NO CHANGE
   B. We had plenty of time before takeoff, so we slowly ate the meal we had bought at the airport.
   C. We had plenty of time before takeoff, so we ate the meal we had bought at the slow airport.
   D. We had plenty of time before takeoff, so we ate the meal we had bought slowly at the airport.

Lesson 16 continued:

Vocabulary: Choosing the Right Use

The following sentences contain vocabulary words used in the reading passage. Identify the sentence or sentences that use the italicized vocabulary word properly. We have changed the form of some vocabulary words to provide new contexts; for example, some adjectives and verbs have been used as nouns.

1) A. *Fluorescent* lighting can make skin tone appear like that of someone who has fallen ill.
   B. The winner of the National Speech Contest won because of the *fluorescent* way she spoke.
   C. Adding *fluorescent* light bulbs to the set of the scary play gave the stage an eerie glow.
   D. Though I could not yet speak Italian *fluorescently*, I knew I could have a basic conversation.

2) A. The invention of the TV remote eliminated the small, operational *nuance* of having to walk across the room to change the channel.
   B. Daniel, always a *nuance*, made whiny noises until Mom agreed to drive him to the toy store.
   C. Our *nuance* of a refrigerator always seems to stop working at the most inconvenient times.
   D. My unreasonable roommate insists that I do not do my share of the cleaning because I neglect insignificant household *nuances* like polishing the trash can.

3) A. Chandler's boss *manipulated* that he buy her a coffee every morning before he arrived at work.
   B. Mrs. Stone *manipulated* excellence from her students, never settling for mediocrity.
   C. Pop star Britney Bright became upset when a magazine editor *manipulated* a photo of her.
   D. Through the remote control unit, Chelsea *manipulated* the arm of the bomb disposal robot, directing it to grasp a suspicious package.

4) A. Please do not arrive to class *contemporary*, as we must begin immediately at 8:00 am.
   B. Reading news on the Internet is the *contemporary* preference, but Grandma still prefers the newspaper and television.
   C. Do you like music from the 1970s, or do you prefer styles that are more *contemporary*?
   D. The *contemporary* child had considerably fewer markers to choose from, as they had all been claimed already.

5) A. Outraged at the article's lazy *typeface*, the editor sent the document back to the writer.
   B. Could you give the phrase "New Product!" a *typeface* that draws more attention, please?
   C. The *typeface* of the comic book captions resembles handwriting even though the text is printed.
   D. The Academy Awards occurs annually and gives out awards based on specific *typefaces* to actors and actresses.

Lesson 16 continued:

6) A. The detective increased the *font* of the image to reveal the face of the person on the security camera video.
B. The bold *font* of the vocabulary words in the reading passages made them easy to identify at a glance.
C. The *font* of the music doesn't appeal to people born after 1988.
D. *Fonts* that seem juvenile or informal should not be used to write your research paper; use Times or Courier instead.

7) A. The *exclusivity* of the racecar increased as the vehicle came upon a steep hill.
B. "Use the accelerator and the brake to change your *exclusivity*," the driving instructor told me.
C. Caitlin's statement, "You can sit with us only if you wear pink," exemplified her clique's *exclusivity*.
D. Most Ivy League colleges practice *exclusivity* and grant admission to only a small percentage of applicants.

8) A. The long, brutal hike up the mountain was a reasonable price to pay for the *superfluous* sunset that awaited us at the top.
B. Joyce's cat had its own room, which many found to be *superfluous*; did one cat really need a whole room to itself?
C. Many teachers considered the new, fancy TV monitors at the school *superfluous* because they barely even used the old ones.
D. Longwood Gardens is home to many fields of unbelievably *superfluous* flowers.

9) A. Who makes a larger *salary* per year—teachers, nurses, or construction workers?
B. Recent graduates often have a difficult time adjusting to the daily ritual of going to their *salaries*.
C. After being fired from her job at the mall, Anna worked hard to find herself a new *salary*.
D. Martin took a decrease in *salary* when he changed jobs, but he enjoyed his new workplace environment much more than the old one.

10) A. When his grades dropped, Arthur's parents had no choice but to *curtail* his TV time.
B. The movie producers decided to *curtail* the film by adding scenes that were previously cut.
C. After *curtailing* her diet to healthy choices only, Aretha discovered that she felt more energized each day.
D. The elementary school's decision to *curtail* recess was well received by the students, who loved to play outside.

Lesson 16 continued:

11) A. To Ellie, who had a passion for art, paying attention in class was *substantial* compared to practicing sketches.
    B. "I have a *substantial* number of questions for you; let's sit down because this might take a while."
    C. "As long as you do your best, whether you win the race or not is *substantial* to me," Coach Drew said to his team.
    D. Ben went to the art store and bought a *substantial* amount of colored parachute cord so that he could make keychain lanyards for all his friends.

Lesson 16 continued:

Synonyms and Antonyms

Match the word with its *antonym*.

1)	curtail	**A.**	inclusion
2)	contemporary	**B.**	old-fashioned
3)	exclusivity	**C.**	insignificant
4)	substantial	**D.**	expand
5)	superfluous	**E.**	necessary

Match the word with its *synonym*.

6)	manipulate	**A.**	light
7)	salary	**B.**	format
8)	fluorescent	**C.**	payment
9)	font	**D.**	control

END
of
LESSON 16

Lesson 17

Questions 12–22 are based on the following passage.

— 1 —

In 2010, after losing his job as a bond trader, Brandon Stanton made a life-altering decision to move to New York City and pursue his interest in photography. He began his journey with an ambitious goal: take pictures of ten thousand New Yorkers and plot them on a map of the city. He would then post these photographs on a blog called *Humans of New York* (HONY).

— 2 —

The HONY { **12** } community, which has grown tremendously in the years after Stanton posted his first image, has been kind and supportive toward Stanton and all of the people photographed. **Empathetic** comments emphasize the humanity of both the subjects of the photos and the audience viewing the pictures, some who, in turn, relate their own stories to { **13** } that of the subjects. { **14** }

12

A) NO CHANGE
B) community, that has grown
C) community which has grown
D) community; that has grown

13

A) NO CHANGE
B) that of themselves
C) those in the subjects
D) those of the subjects

14

The content of paragraph 2 interrupts the flow of the passage. Paragraph 2 should be relocated to

A) precede paragraph 1, as the introduction.
B) follow paragraph 3.
C) follow paragraph 4.
D) follow paragraph 5.

Lesson 17 continued:

— 3 —

[1] Armed only with a camera and a **{ 15 }** congenital smile, Stanton approached strangers on the street. [2] He tended to gravitate toward **vibrant**-looking individuals, children, and people whose eyes had a story to tell. [3] **{ 16 }** Stantons' project soon transformed as he interacted with the subjects of his images. [4] Instead of sharing only **candid** photos, Stanton started to include snippets of conversations he had with empathetic people. [5] Stanton prefers to use a Canon camera with a 50mm lens. [6] These **captions** started out simple enough and usually included an element of humor, such as "bystanders wondering why a man was running into traffic with a camera." [7] **{ 17 }** As popularity was gained by Stanton's blog, and he grew in confidence, the captions became more thought provoking. [8] He would ask his subjects about their biggest fears, happiest moments, and **{ 18 }** their memories they considered the worst. [9] In spite of the fact that they were talking to someone they didn't know, or perhaps because of it, the people would share incredibly personal stories with Stanton and, by extension, everyone in the community who read his blog. **{ 19 }**

15

A) NO CHANGE
B) congenial
C) cognitive
D) congruous

16

A) NO CHANGE
B) Stantons' Project
C) Stanton's project
D) Stantons's project

17

Choose the best revision for the underlined portion of the sentence.

A) As Stanton grew confident and his blog gained popularity
B) As popularity began to be gained by Stanton's blog, and Stanton became confident
C) As Stanton grew confident, and popularity was gained by the blog
D) As Stanton's blog gained popularity and confidence for Stanton

18

A) NO CHANGE
B) their worst memories
C) worst memories
D) the memories they considered worst

19

The writer wants to eliminate a sentence that doesn't contribute substantially to the passage. Which sentence would be the best to delete?

A) sentence [2]
B) sentence [3]
C) sentence [4]
D) sentence [5]

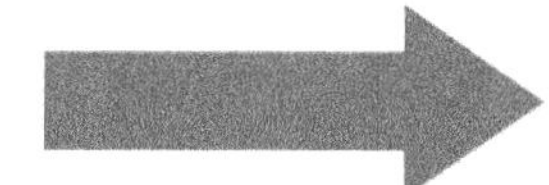

LANGUAGE PASSAGE

Lesson 17 continued:

— 4 —

With the involvement of the online community, Stanton has expanded his blog beyond casual photojournalism. In January 2015, Stanton photographed a middle-schooler who said that his principal, Ms. Lopez, influenced him most in his life. Stanton followed up with Ms. Lopez, who lamented how budget cuts had negatively affected the school, which was a safe **haven** for children living in a high-crime area. Together, Stanton and Ms. Lopez discussed how the HONY community could help **actualize** the school's vision. They set up an online fundraiser to send neighborhood children on a tour of Harvard University. Within a week, over fifty thousand people had donated more than $1 million to the fundraiser. The **{ 20 }** money, that has been used for both future tours of Harvard and a scholarship fund, exceeded expectations.

— 5 —

This example of **philanthropy** illustrates how Stanton's initial idea of creating a photographic census has been transformed into an entity that is much greater than its initial concept. The *Humans of New York* blog fosters a connection between people. It not only tells the stories of the people in the pictures in a neat, **unobtrusive** way, **{ 21 }** but they also reminds viewers that all the strangers they pass on the street have struggles and fears, hopes and dreams, just like they do. **{ 22 }**

20

A) NO CHANGE
B) money, which
C) money; that
D) money which

21

A) NO CHANGE
B) but they too
C) but it also
D) and they also

22

The writer would like to add a concluding sentence at this point. Choose the most appropriate sentence to insert here.

A) As it turns out, HONY is a better charity than it is a blog.
B) HONY is more than simple photography—it is a window to the soul.
C) Through HONY, Stanton's photography has captured the essence of humanity.
D) This, in addition to the other elements, makes HONY truly bigger than a simple photo blog.

Lesson 17 continued:

Vocabulary: Context Answers

The following sentences contain vocabulary words used in the reading passage. Choose the answer that best completes the sentence. There may be more than one technically correct answer, but one will better exemplify the italicized vocabulary word than the others will.

1) Kelly was glad to have an *empathetic* teacher that she knew would _____.
   A. refer her to a counselor
   B. help her solve her problems
   C. not ask about her problems
   D. understand how she felt
   E. let her come late to class

2) The young actor hoped that her *vibrant* personality would shine through in the audition; she wanted to show the casting director that she was _____.
   A. young and naïve
   B. energetic and enthusiastic
   C. serious and hard-working
   D. uncomfortable and worried
   E. easy-going and funny

3) Javon _____, but the *candid* picture turned out surprisingly well.
   A. had an old camera
   B. was not expecting to be photographed
   C. was not a professional photographer
   D. waited a long time to get his photos developed
   E. had trouble finding inspiration

4) Without the *captions* _____, the photojournalism class could not follow the story.
   A. keeping the pictures in order
   B. explaining the photographs
   C. instructing the students
   D. and their own background knowledge
   E. that they wrote

5) The _____ served as a *haven* for local animals.
   A. house
   B. poultry factory
   C. construction site
   D. lumber yard
   E. wildlife refuge

6) Without funding, the nonprofit could never *actualize* their goals; they can _____ if they do not have support.
   A. accomplish their dreams
   B. never meet their objectives
   C. not get funding
   D. grow in size
   E. not correct their opponents

7) *Philanthropy* is an important part of the school's mission, which is why it created a basketball tournament to _____.
   A. raise money for pediatric cancer
   B. give students something fun to do
   C. test the new gymnasium
   D. raise money for the basketball team
   E. find the best team in the county

8) Though the tattoo was relatively *unobtrusive*, Betty knew that her mother's _____.
   A. conservative ideas would forbid it
   B. hawk-like eyes would see it immediately
   C. concern was warranted
   D. aging vision would miss it completely
   E. free-spirited nature would appreciate it

Lesson 17 continued:

Writing Practice

The underlined portion of each sentence possibly contains an error related to the use of restrictive and nonrestrictive clauses. Select the answer that best corrects the flaw. Select NO CHANGE if the underlined portion is correct.

1) The little boy cried when the toy, that he had had for months, broke.
   A. NO CHANGE
   B. toy, that he had had for months;
   C. toy, which he had had for months
   D. toy, which he had had for months,

2) The one author who had been invited to speak declined to do so.
   A. NO CHANGE
   B. author, who had been invited to speak, declined
   C. author, who had been invited to speak declined,
   D. author, that had been invited to speak declined,

3) The bedroom which has just been painted is down the hall.
   A. NO CHANGE
   B. The bedroom, which has just been painted, is
   C. The bedroom which has just been painted, is
   D. The bedroom, which has just been painted is,

4) The fan I met at the basketball game, was wearing the jersey of my favorite player.
   A. NO CHANGE
   B. The fan, who I met at the basketball game was
   C. The fan, I met at the basketball game, was
   D. The fan I met at the basketball game was

5) That pound of chocolate which probably has a million calories in it was very tempting.
   A. NO CHANGE
   B. That pound of chocolate, which probably has a million calories in it, was very tempting.
   C. That pound of chocolate, that probably has a million calories in it, was very tempting.
   D. That pound of chocolate which probably has a million calories in it, was very tempting.

Lesson 17 continued:

6) Last night, the entire senior class went to see the <u>movie that had just been filmed in our hometown.</u>
   A. NO CHANGE
   B. movie, that had just been filmed, in our hometown.
   C. movie that had just been filmed, in our hometown.
   D. movie which had just been filmed in our hometown.

7) <u>Everyone who dresses up for Halloween is eligible</u> to participate in the "Best Costume" contest before trick-or-treating begins.
   A. NO CHANGE
   B. Everyone, who dresses up for Halloween is eligible,
   C. Everyone who dresses up for Halloween, is eligible
   D. Everyone, who dresses up for Halloween, is eligible

8) <u>The *USS Missouri* a ship that was instrumental in various battles during WWII also</u> served in the Korean War.
   A. NO CHANGE
   B. The *USS Missouri*, a ship that was instrumental in various battles during WWII, also
   C. The *USS Missouri*, a ship that was instrumental in various battles during WWII also
   D. The *USS Missouri* a ship that was instrumental in various battles during WWII, also

9) <u>Kofi Annan who was the Secretary General of the United Nations from 1997 to 2006 has spent much of his adult life working for peace in lands that have not known it for many years.</u>
   A. NO CHANGE
   B. Kofi Annan, who was the Secretary General of the United Nations, from 1997 to 2006 has spent much of his adult life working for peace in lands, that have not known it for many years.
   C. Kofi Annan, who was the Secretary General of the United Nations from 1997 to 2006, has spent much of his adult life working for peace in lands that have not known it for many years.
   D. Kofi Annan who was the Secretary General of the United Nations from 1997 to 2006 has spent much of his adult life working for peace in lands, that have not known it, for many years.

10) <u>There is a well-known phrase, that satirizes the way philosophy operates in the real world: When confronted by two theories, choose the one, which is funnier.</u>
   A. NO CHANGE
   B. There is a well-known phrase that satirizes the way philosophy operates in the real world: When confronted by two theories, choose the one that is funnier.
   C. There is a well-known phrase, that satirizes the way philosophy operates, in the real world: When confronted by two theories, choose the one, which is funnier.
   D. There is a well-known phrase, which satirizes the way philosophy operates in the real world: When confronted by two theories, choose the one which is funnier.

Lesson 17 continued:

Vocabulary: Choosing the Right Use

The following sentences contain vocabulary words used in the reading passage. Identify the sentence or sentences that use the italicized vocabulary word properly. We have changed the form of some vocabulary words to provide new contexts; for example, some adjectives and verbs have been used as nouns.

1) A. Kyle was so *empathetic* for his upcoming birthday party that he hopped up and down as his parents hung streamers.
   B. Having been widowed a year ago, Charlotte was especially *empathetic* towards Mrs. Seong after her husband's funeral.
   C. When Max felt upset after his girlfriend broke up with him, his friends were *empathetic* and comforted him.
   D. Phoebe was exhausted when she finished work, but her *empathetic* dog raced around the apartment because it needed a walk.

2) A. Cindy has a *vibrant* personality; her laughter and high spirits are infectious to those around her.
   B. Traffic came to a standstill after a *vibrant* car accident; both vehicles were totaled, but luckily, the drivers had only minor injuries.
   C. Zoo visitors were impressed by the peacock's *vibrant* blue and green plumage as it displayed its feathers.
   D. The park ranger warned hikers that the grizzly bears could be *vibrant* and attack to protect their young.

3) A. The photographer took a great deal of *candid* pictures of the wedding party, while the bride and groom prepared for the ceremony.
   B. The art historian was impressed by the still-life painting that the *candid* artist had skillfully created with careful brush strokes.
   C. The sculptor was famous for his *candid* skills; every marble sculpture was beautifully carved.
   D. Karen felt embarrassed by the *candid* photograph her dad took as she was blowing out the candles on her cake.

4) A. Journalists will often write *captions* of new movies they have seen or book series they have read.
   B. The Broadway performance received mixed *captions*; some critics adored it, and some simply did not understand the point of it.
   C. The *caption* identifies the man standing on the left as the founder of the new technology company.
   D. In the news article, the original source of the photograph is cited in the *caption* just below the image.

Lesson 17 continued:

5) A. The *congenial* neighbors introduced themselves and brought over a casserole when the Turner family moved in.
   B. Diane, who feared dogs, cast a *congenial* look at the dozing golden retriever as she walked past it.
   C. The store owner kept a *congenial* eye on the three rough-housing boys who nearly knocked over a shelf.
   D. When Sandy saw her old friend Pete at the grocery store, the pair had a *congenial* conversation.

6) A. At the restaurant, Dylan always orders the chocolate cake; he says the delicious dessert tastes like *haven*.
   B. Emily likes going to the stream in the woods; it is a quiet *haven* where she can take a break from her parents and the pressures of school.
   C. After weeks of dangerous travels, the refugees finally reached a *haven* far away from the war.
   D. Although the teenager was not religious, she believed that people go to *haven* when they pass away.

7) A. The president's plan to build a highway across the nation took years to *actualize*, but once it was complete, travel became easier.
   B. Nate wanted to *actualize* his paper before turning it in, so he corrected typos and rewrote a poorly worded paragraph.
   C. When Travis decided to collect food for the local homeless people, the community helped him *actualize* his goal by donating canned goods.
   D. Marie was a good basketball player because she spent weeks practicing in order to *actualize* her athletic abilities.

8) A. The *philanthropy* of the celebrity's party, which included a full orchestra, amazed the guests.
   B. As a final act of *philanthropy*, the elderly man requested that his estate be turned into an orphanage.
   C. Charles spends all of his money on *philanthropy*, buying flashy, tailored suits and fancy sports cars.
   D. The billionaire was known for his *philanthropy* and started a foundation that works to end global poverty.

9) A. Because the class was taking a test, the principal tried to be *unobtrusive* as he quietly spoke with the teacher.
   B. The *unobtrusive* arrival of her father-in-law stressed Laura, who had not even had time to prepare the guest room.
   C. The rainstorm, though brief, had been *unobtrusive*, because the meteorologist had predicted clear skies.
   D. The *unobtrusive* custodian cleaned the office in the evening, after the other employees went home.

Lesson 17 continued:

Synonyms and Antonyms

Match the word with its *antonym*.

1) empathetic **A.** noticeable

2) unobtrusive **B.** dull

3) candid **C.** indifferent

4) vibrant **D.** posed

Match the word with its *synonym*.

5) caption **A.** explanation

6) actualize **B.** charity

7) philanthropy **C.** sanctuary

8) haven **D.** realize

END of LESSON 17

Lesson 18

Questions 23–33 are based on the following passage.

— 1 —

{ **23** } For decades government officials, environmentalists, and citizens of California have recognized the **inevitability** of a drought as one of the hazards { **24** } to live in a desert region that endures exceptionally dry years. In 2012, the drought reached proportions beyond what many people had expected; in fact, it was the worst drought in California's history. { **25** } Reservoirs not only are shrinking, but also, and more significantly, the aquifers are being depleted at dangerously fast rates. **Aquifers**, groundwater sources beneath the surface, are an important source of reserved water. Under normal circumstances, aquifers are gradually refilled by precipitation, rivers, and snowmelt, but in recent years, there has not been enough surface water to restore the aquifers. This **depletion** of groundwater could have profound effects on the geology of the area, including even drops in land elevation.

— 2 —

[1] A number of factors have led to California's record drought. [2] Weather conditions have caused California to experience little precipitation, even during the typically wet winters. [3] Warmer temperatures have caused increased evaporation rates, **exacerbating** the problem. [4] Seasonal weather, unfortunately, cannot be predicted. [5] According to the National Weather Service, these weather and climate factors have rendered the drought the worst since 1895. [6] Of course, in 1895, an extreme drought had limited consequences. [7] The population of California has grown from about 1.5 million people in { **26** } nineteen hundred to about 37 million people in 2010; in the past fifty years alone, the population has more { **27** } then doubled. [8] Technology and transportation might have increased in that time, but nature's water supply, however, has not. { **28** }

23

A) NO CHANGE
B) For decades:
C) For decades,
D) For decades—

24

A) NO CHANGE
B) of to live in a desert
C) of life of a desert
D) of living in a desert

25

A) NO CHANGE
B) Not only are reservoirs shrinking,
C) Reservoirs are shrinking not only,
D) Reservoirs are, not only shrinking,

26

A) NO CHANGE
B) 1,900
C) 1900
D) Nineteen hundred

27

A) NO CHANGE
B) by doubled
C) then multiplied
D) than doubled

28

The writer wants to delete a sentence that does not contribute to paragraph 2. Choose the best sentence to delete.

A) sentence [4]
B) sentence [5]
C) sentence [6]
D) sentence [7]

Lesson 18 continued:

— 3 —

[1] To make matters { **29** } worst, California is the country's largest agricultural supplier, growing half of the fruits and vegetables in the United States. [2] The agricultural industry depends on irrigation. [3] Roughly eighty percent of California's developed water supply goes toward agriculture, while the remaining twenty percent is for urban use. [4] Although there is less surface water available, farmers still have to irrigate { **30** } they're crops, so they pump groundwater. [5] Pumping groundwater for crops is not bad when precipitation replaces the supply, but in times of drought, the whole state depends on groundwater. [6] Replacing lost rainwater with groundwater is a short-term solution that could cause significant problems in the future. [7] Dependence on water from aquifers can lead to groundwater **overdraft** and its numerous **detrimental** effects, such as the drops in land elevation. [8] A **hydrologist** with the US Geological Survey has found that San Joaquin Valley is already sinking at a foot a year. [9] Due to the geology of the aquifers, the sinking, or **subsidence**, is { **31** } permanent which means that the aquifers, in turn, are shrinking in capacity. [10] Pumping groundwater as a temporary solution also threatens the state's ability to withstand droughts in the future. [11] The government of California is working to solve the water crisis. [12] In 2015, Governor Jerry Brown announced the state's first mandatory water restrictions. [13] The restrictions require cities and towns to reduce water usage by twenty-five percent; however, { **32** } because only urban areas account for twenty percent of water use, these measures are not as drastic as they might seem. [14] The state legislature has approved restrictions on groundwater pumping for agriculture, but these measures will be gradually phased in between 2020 and 2040. [15] This legislation is a step in the right direction, but it may prove to be too little too late. { **33** }

29

A) NO CHANGE
B) worst: California
C) worse, California
D) more worse, California

30

A) NO CHANGE
B) their
C) theyre
D) there

31

A) NO CHANGE
B) permanent, that means
C) permanent; which means
D) permanent, which means

32

A) NO CHANGE
B) since urban areas only account for only twenty percent
C) because urban areas account for only twenty percent
D) since urban areas only account for 20 percent

33

The writer wants to divide paragraph 3 into two paragraphs. Choose the point at which the new paragraph should begin.

A) sentence [6]
B) sentence [8]
C) sentence [11]
D) sentence [12]

Lesson 18 continued:

Vocabulary: Context Answers

The following sentences contain vocabulary words used in the reading passage. Choose the answer that best completes the sentence. There may be more than one technically correct answer, but one will better exemplify the italicized vocabulary word than the others will.

1) Peter knew _____; the *inevitability* of performing poorly on an exam was clear from the beginning.
   A. he would eventually fail
   B. he would always pass
   C. he might not pass
   D. the tests were easy
   E. a passing grade was achievable

2) *Aquifers* store _____ and are an important resource for farmers.
   A. water in tanks
   B. crops in silos
   C. fertilizer in barns
   D. water in the ground
   E. water in troughs

3) During the unexpectedly long flood, a *depletion* of supplies left families _____.
   A. with wet, ruined rations
   B. happy for the time being
   C. with food to share
   D. with more resources than necessary
   E. without enough food

4) Now that Wendy was finally safe and able to rest, her health was _____ without fatigue *exacerbating* her ailments.
   A. perfect
   B. improving
   C. regressing
   D. awful
   E. the same

5) The twins' constant demands were an *overdraft* on Stacy's patience, and, by the end of the day, she _____.
   A. was calm, but tired
   B. shouted at the least provocation
   C. was glad to go to bed
   D. remained collected and reasonable
   E. had all the chores finished

6) Access to the Internet proved to be *detrimental* to the study group's focus: they were ______.
   A. much more productive than they usually were
   B. using the Internet to do their work
   C. unable able to get any work done
   D. unable to access the Internet when they needed it
   E. excited to get started

7) Ever since Judy _____ as a young girl, she knew she wanted to study to become a *hydrologist.*
   A. caught a fish
   B. went to the dentist
   C. visited a farm
   D. learned to garden
   E. saw the ocean

8) *Subsidence* forced the Ratcliff family to renovate their home after the _____ cracked the building's foundation.
   A. mudslide
   B. sinking elevation
   C. flooding
   D. rising sea level
   E. house's weight

Lesson 18 continued:

Writing Practice

The following sentences contain words that are often misused. Choose the correct word in each sentence.

1) After I came home yesterday, I laid / lay my coat over the back of the chair.

2) The front-row tickets laid / lay safely on the kitchen counter.

3) Please make sure to set / sit all the cushions on the couch nicely.

4) Before George left for college, his parents sat / set down with him and discussed finances.

5) The sun raised / rose bright and golden over the Rocky Mountains.

6) The new TV show portrays zombies that are able to raise / rise themselves out of their graves.

7) I hope it isn't much farther / further to the airport.

8) Denise hurt my feelings farther / further than ever before.

9) The government banned cigarette ads from TV: The explicit / implicit message is "Don't smoke."

10) I told you explicitly / implicitly not to bother the dog!

11) I couldn't see any differences among / between the climates of Mexico, Honduras, and Belize.

12) There is no doubt: Among / Between Pepsi and Coke, Pepsi is sweeter.

13) Is it a good idea to assure / ensure / insure everyone that they will get a part in the play?

Lesson 18 continued:

Vocabulary: Choosing the Right Use

The following sentences contain vocabulary words used in the reading passage. Identify the sentence or sentences that use the italicized vocabulary word properly. We have changed the form of some vocabulary words to provide new contexts; for example, some adjectives and verbs have been used as nouns.

1) A. Sam recognized the *inevitability* of drifting apart from his classmates when they left their small town to attend different colleges.
   B. Officials conveyed the *inevitability* of drunk driving, which can kill motorists, and urged people to stay off the roads if they were not sober.
   C. Nearby residents were concerned about the *inevitability* of the wildfire that was only partially contained by fire crews.
   D. Though getting old is an *inevitability*, countless cosmetic products claim to stop the aging process.

2) A. The local children like to swim in the nearby *aquifer* that fills with rainwater and snowmelt in the summer.
   B. The wildlife service relocated the *aquifer* so the caribou would have better access to the mountain pass.
   C. Western Tennessee has high-quality drinking water that is drawn from the underground *aquifer*.
   D. Geologists worried that the *aquifer* could be polluted if the proposed oil well were to leak.

3) A. The accidental *depletion* of his finished essay frustrated Carl; now he would have to rewrite the entire paper.
   B. Anna was surprised by the rapid *depletion* of her phone battery; it was charged last night, but her brother had secretly played games on it.
   C. Environmentalists warned that the *depletion* of the rain forests could endanger countless plants and animals and affect the atmosphere on a global scale.
   D. Jane's *depletion* of online friends who made her feel bad vastly improved her experiences on social media.

4) A. The inexperienced doctor *exacerbated* the patient's condition when he administered the wrong medicine.
   B. The young children *exacerbated* their mother by running inside the house and yelling loudly.
   C. At the family reunion, Ralph found his niece *exacerbating* the cat by pulling on its tail.
   D. Traffic often slowed where the highway split, and the additional holiday travelers were *exacerbating* the problem.

5) A. The strong *overdraft* on the stormy day blew the man's umbrella inside out.
   B. The bank charged Jaime a penalty fee for *overdraft* after she spent more money than she had in her checking account.
   C. Excessive irrigation caused the *overdraft* of well water, so local residents had virtually no water available.
   D. The pilot cautioned passengers to buckle their seatbelts because the *overdraft* would cause turbulence.

Lesson 18 continued:

6) A. A *detrimental* delay to the opening of the play caused audience members to wonder why the curtains were still closed.
   B. Bruce's career as a rock musician was *detrimental* to his hearing, and he is now partially deaf in both ears.
   C. Doctors advise that smoking is *detrimental* to one's health and can cause cancer and other health problems.
   D. Melissa fell off her bicycle, but received only *detrimental* injuries that did not even bleed.

7) A. When the river near the town started to dry up for no apparent reason, the mayor consulted with a *hydrologist*.
   B. The *hydrologist* was able to determine the approximate age of the rocks that jutted from the earth's surface.
   C. Moon rocks are of interest to *hydrologists*, who determine how the elemental and mineral makeup of the moon differs from that of Earth.
   D. A *hydrologist* visited the elementary school class and explained how the water cycle works.

8) A. The building's gradual *subsidence* was a result of the soft, marshy ground it was built upon.
   B. The professor stated that while the paper was well written, it lacked *subsidence* and did not make a compelling argument.
   C. Scientists noted the *subsidence* of the mountain after the earthquake; the landform was now shorter, on average, by seven feet.
   D. When handling the hazardous *subsidence*, chemists wear protective gear and use special tools.

Lesson 18 continued:

Synonyms and Antonyms

Match the word with its *antonym*.

1)	detrimental	**A.**	improve
2)	subsidence	**B.**	rise
3)	depletion	**C.**	beneficial
4)	exacerbate	**D.**	increase

Match the word with its *synonym*.

5)	inevitability	**A.**	certainty
6)	overdraft	**B.**	basin
7)	aquifer	**C.**	exhaustion

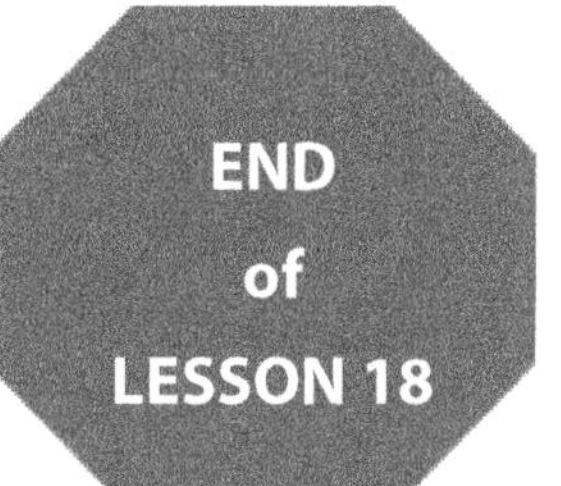

Lesson 19

Questions 34–44 are based on the following passage.

— 1 —

[1] Every day, for over ten years, at least one or two Americans have orbited Earth on the International Space Station (ISS). [2] Space research has become so normalized that few people even think about the people from the United States, Canada, Europe, Japan, and Russia, floating miles above their homes. [3] Launched in 1998, the spacefaring port is about the size of a 6-bedroom house. [4] As of 2015, more than 200 astronauts and cosmonauts have lived in space amid the dark, lethal **void**, in relative isolation. [5] Crew members, in spite of their different nationalities and cultures, generally get along well, or at least better than they get along with Mission Control. [6] Some American astronauts have spent more than a year living there. **{ 34 } { 35 }**

— 2 —

NASA and other space agencies monitor astronauts' mental health just as much as they monitor their physical health. Astronauts have private conversations with NASA psychologists every two weeks, with the option to talk to them **{ 36 }** more. This ensures that psychologists can help those on the Space Station cope with issues that come up. Researchers also keep track of their emotional health in personal ways; from 2003 to 2010, ten Americans kept **anonymous** diaries for **anthropologist** Jack Stuster, who studies people who live in extreme conditions. These diaries provide more casual, and perhaps more revealing, insights into the minds of the astronauts. **{ 37 }** As expected, the diaries reveal the **spectrum** of emotions one would expect: excitement to be in space, boredom from repetitive activities, and occasional frustration over minor and major things, the most common being the Station's relationship with Mission Control.

34

The author is considering adding a sentence at this point. Choose the most appropriate sentence to insert.

A) They orbit at a speed of 17,000 mph, which sounds extreme, but they don't even notice.
B) Who wouldn't want to live there, at least for a little while, like for a few weeks?
C) It costs NASA $71 million to send each astronaut there, leaving people to wonder why launches are so expensive.
D) This leads many to wonder just how living in space affects one's emotional and mental health.

35

Choose the sentence that should be relocated to paragraph 4.

A) sentence [1]
B) sentence [3]
C) sentence [5]
D) sentence [6]

36

A) NO CHANGE
B) more if needed. This ensures
C) more frequently: this ensures
D) more, this ensures

37

A) NO CHANGE
B) The
C) Like you would guess, the
D) Typically, the

Lesson 19 continued:

— 3 —

Mission Control { **38** } with the International Space Station maintain a complex **rapport**. The Station, unlike a shuttle on a relatively short, specific mission, offers some limited independence. Each morning, the Station must radio Mission Control and then sign off at night, and, as a rule, Mission Control avoids disturbing the { **39** } astronauts like the plague in their off hours unless absolutely necessary. That is about the extent of the crew's independence; the astronauts have little **autonomy** with regards to their missions. They follow strict schedules developed by ground control and mapped out on spreadsheets. When an astronaut clicks on a time block on an ISS computer, it expands to detail the procedure that must be completed at that moment and all of the necessary steps that need to be followed. Some tasks have as many as four hundred steps! During a task, a red line moves across the screen, indicating what the astronaut should be doing at any given moment. Astronaut Garrett Reisman once complained, "The red line, no matter what I do, it just keeps moving to the right. I can't { **40** } stop it"! The scheduling is made more stressful because of the occasional disconnect between the Station and Mission Control. Astronauts have been **allotted** thirty minutes for projects that actually required over three hours to complete. Crew members have complained that Mission Control does not understand what life in space is like.

38

A) NO CHANGE
B) by
C) and
D) along

39

A) NO CHANGE
B) astronauts
C) astronauts, like they're the plague
D) plagued astronauts

40

A) NO CHANGE
B) stop it".
C) stop it"
D) stop it!"

Lesson 19 continued:

— 4 —

Not surprisingly, psychologists have reported tension between the two groups. Researchers have found that over time, an isolated crew would decrease interactions with Mission Control, a behavior termed "psychological closing." Crew members have even viewed some ground control personnel as opponents or { **41** } rivals, in one incident, the crew turned off their radios and ignored NASA for an entire day. This deliberate **severing** of communication highlights both the physical and emotional distance between the units. These disruptive and sometimes **discordant** interactions are almost exclusively between Mission Control and the astronauts. Cosmonauts and astronauts usually stay in their separate modules during the workday, but gather together at mealtimes and watch movies together on Fridays, fostering a sense of group **cohesion**. Most of the time, the crew members are almost completely isolated as they work alone or in groups of one or two. NASA tries to alleviate the constant strain of isolation by allowing astronauts to communicate with family and friends on Earth whenever they have the opportunity. Internet access { **42** } from 2010 ensures they can have video or voice chats with family and ground control. { **43** } Emotionally, long, six-month trips wear down astronauts, but communication helps to mitigate the effects and up morale.

— 5 —

Living in space also has positive effects on crew members' emotional health. Watching the inspiring majesty of your home planet from orbit never gets old. Upon returning from space, crew members report higher levels of appreciation for people and nature, spirituality, and power. { **44** } While the negative affects of isolation are temporary, these positive emotional changes are likely to be permanent. This potential change indicates that while space crews still need to improve communication to stave off loneliness or hostility, time on the International Space Station is beneficial for emotional and mental health overall.

41

A) NO CHANGE
B) rivals. In one incident, the crew
C) rivals, in one incident. The crew
D) rivals, in one incident; the crew

42

A) NO CHANGE
B) in
C) available
D) made available in

43

Choose the best revision for the underlined sentence.

A) Long, six-month trips wear astronauts emotionally down, but communication helps to reduce the effects of low morale.
B) Six month trips, long, wear down astronauts emotionally, but communication helps improve morale.
C) Long, six-month trips wear down astronauts emotionally, but communication helps to improve morale.
D) Astronauts wear down emotionally from six-month trips, which are long, but morale is improved by communication.

44

A) NO CHANGE
B) effects
C) affect's
D) effects'

Lesson 19 continued:

Vocabulary: Context Answers

The following sentences contain vocabulary words used in the reading passage. Choose the answer that best completes the sentence. There may be more than one technically correct answer, but one will better exemplify the italicized vocabulary word than the others will.

1) The deep well looked like a bottomless *void*, _____.
   A. damp and loud
   B. quiet and peaceful
   C. dark and infinite
   D. large and echoing
   E. bright and shining

2) _____ the *anonymous* love letter that she received.
   A. Everyone was sure who sent
   B. No one knew who sent
   C. Eric had signed
   D. The entire class read
   E. Quinn confronted the person who sent

3) Erin's _____ class was taught by a professional *anthropologist*.
   A. Prehistoric Wildlife
   B. Insect Anatomy
   C. Performance and Acrobatics
   D. Prehistoric Human Society
   E. Calculus

4) Throughout the day, Gary felt a *spectrum* of emotions that varied _____.
   A. widely
   B. very little
   C. on a scale from ecstatic to depressed
   D. between fixed points
   E. incomprehensibly

5) Sharon's new group _____; she longed for the *rapport* that her previous group had had.
   A. was extremely efficient
   B. completed their assignments ahead of time
   C. did not work together very well
   D. was very considerate
   E. did all of their work independently

6) Since learning to drive, Kaitlyn had a sense of *autonomy* that also made her very _____ when her mother told her to clean her room.
   A. defiant
   B. agreeable
   C. angry
   D. upset
   E. relaxed

Lesson 19 continued:

7) The proctor *allotted* students two pencils each with which to complete the exam; Doreen thought she would need more than _____.
   A. she had needed for the last test
   B. her classmates would
   C. what was left at the proctor's desk
   D. had been distributed to her
   E. one eraser

8) It was difficult to do, but Andrea felt that *severing* all contact with her ex-boyfriend was for the best; now, she _____.
   A. remained friends with him
   B. did not hear from him at all
   C. saw him around town
   D. spoke with him frequently
   E. invited him out with her friends

9) John and Jim's *discordant* relationship make it difficult for them to run a business together because they never _____.
   A. make any decisions
   B. discuss their jobs
   C. have any arguments
   D. agree on anything
   E. see each other

10) The coach created a sense of *cohesion* within the soccer team by _____.
   A. favoring individual players over others
   B. discussing strategy as a group
   C. letting the captains be in charge
   D. allowing players to make their own decisions
   E. using practice drills

11) Heather's doctor hopes to *mitigate* the swelling in her ankle with ice and rest; without this treatment, the swelling _____.
   A. will disperse
   B. could continue
   C. will only increase
   D. should decrease
   E. will hurt

Lesson 19 continued:

Writing Practice

The following sentences contain words that are often misused. Choose the correct word in each sentence.

1) You need to assure / ensure / insure that the dog is friendly before buying it.

2) Mr. Carmine read the poem and tried to elicit / illicit some favorable responses to it.

3) Constant and elicit / illicit drug use throughout the neighborhood caught the attention of the police.

4) Earlier, emigration / immigration to the United States came mostly from Europe.

5) Every year, people spend fewer / less time watching scheduled TV shows.

6) People read fewer / less books for pleasure than they used to.

7) From the speech, reporters were able to imply / infer that the mayor's campaign needed money.

8) The author's harsh tone implies / infers that she has personal experience in the subject.

9) It's / Its nothing; don't mention it. I'll be happy to walk your dog and fix it's / its food.

10) "My job, sir, is to advice / advise you on important matters," said the minister.

11) Irregardless / Regardless of your belief that UFOs exist, I think what you saw was an airplane.

12) Sometimes / Some times, a rainbow appears over the hill.

13) Rachel wanted to work on the project everyday / every day until it was finished.

Lesson 19 continued:

Vocabulary: Choosing the Right Use

The following sentences contain vocabulary words used in the reading passage. Identify the sentence or sentences that use the italicized vocabulary word properly. We have changed the form of some vocabulary words to provide new contexts; for example, some adjectives and verbs have been used as nouns.

1) A. In the science fiction movie, the alien spaceship was pulled into the *void* of a black hole, never to be seen again.
   B. Many frogs and toads live in the *void* during the summer when the current is not strong.
   C. In the *void* of a vacuum, a feather and a baseball will fall at exactly the same rate because there is no air resistance.
   D. Construction workers used a backhoe to dig a *void* for rainwater to flow into so the area would not flood.

2) A. When Rachel saw her former teacher at the bookstore, they had an *anonymous* conversation about the class.
   B. With *anonymous* surveys, students can rate their professor without worrying that it could affect their grades.
   C. The students' *anonymous* homework assignments were graded for completion, not for correct answers.
   D. Because he wanted to remain *anonymous*, the writer did not sign his name in the letter to the editor.

3) A. The *anthropologist* studied the distant star system through a powerful telescope.
   B. A number of *anthropologists* have traveled to Indonesia to study the various island cultures.
   C. Though wary at first, the Native Americans allowed the *anthropologist* onto the reservation to observe their customs.
   D. As the spacecraft entered Jupiter's orbit, the *anthropologists* celebrated and excitedly waited for detailed images of the planet.

4) A. A glass prism can separate a beam of white light into a *spectrum* of all the colors of the rainbow.
   B. As the toddler started to have a tantrum at the restaurant, her father urged her not to create a *spectrum*.
   C. Most audience members thought that the man who had stormed on stage to interrupt the award recipient's speech was making a *spectrum* of himself.
   D. The president's proposal was met with a *spectrum* of opinions, from full support to calls for impeachment.

5) A. After the battle, the lieutenant sent a *rapport* that documented what happened to his commanding officer.
   B. Tyler had procrastinated, so now, he must rush to write his *rapport* on World War I the night before the due date.
   C. The boss maintained a good *rapport* with the employees by occasionally having lunch with them.
   D. Therapists need to establish a *rapport* with their patients in order to most effectively help them.

Lesson 19 continued:

6) A. As children grow older, they want increasing *autonomy* and the right to make their own decisions.
   B. In biology class, the students learned about the *autonomy* of frogs by dissecting them.
   C. Some residents of Texas want their state to gain full *autonomy* and not be under the control of the federal government.
   D. The mechanic explained the *autonomy* of the car to his niece, telling her what the parts do and how they fit together.

7) A. After the disaster, the blood bank encouraged people to *allot* blood to help the injured victims.
   B. Walter *allotted* his granddaughters five dollars each to spend in the candy store and told them to buy whatever they wanted.
   C. Having little money, Andy *allotted* his mom a loving hug and a bouquet of wildflowers on Mother's Day.
   D. The class had only three days to make their science presentations, so the teacher *allotted* ten minutes for each student to speak.

8) A. Because her plant had started to rot, Lisa had to *sever* the healthy portion from the dying stem in hopes that it could grow roots.
   B. The star track athlete easily *severed* the other runners and won the race with a four-yard lead.
   C. The football player signaled his teammate to *sever* the ball to him so he could score a touchdown.
   D. When Ashley realized that her friend was a bully, she *severed* all ties with him and did not even speak to him at school.

9) A. The instructor, though friendly, was *discordant* and often misplaced papers and lecture notes.
   B. Audience members grimaced at the *discordant* sounds the middle school band made while tuning.
   C. Mr. and Mrs. Smith called a family meeting so the *discordant* children could settle their ongoing argument.
   D. The child drew a stick through an ant trail, which caused the insects to become *discordant* and scatter.

10) A. There was *cohesion* at the theater when the fire alarms sounded and everyone had to evacuate.
    B. To avoid any *cohesion* about the project, the teacher printed clear instructions that detailed how it would be graded.
    C. Although the movie has good effects, it lacks *cohesion* because it jumps between scenes at random.
    D. Fans are impressed by the *cohesion* of the band; after twenty years, the original members remain close friends and still tour together.

11) A. Emergency funds and disaster relief agencies *mitigated* the suffering of the people displaced by the flood.
    B. While organizing his digital files, Ian *mitigated* documents on the computer desktop to appropriate folders.
    C. The doctor prescribed the patient medicine that *mitigated* the worst of the flu symptoms.
    D. Animal control *mitigated* the bear from the suburban neighborhood to a mountainous forest.

Lesson 19 continued:

Synonyms and Antonyms

Match the word with its *antonym*.

1)	anonymous	**A.**	dependence
2)	autonomy	**B.**	harmonious
3)	mitigate	**C.**	connect
4)	sever	**D.**	known
5)	discordant	**E.**	worsen

Match the word with its *synonym*.

6)	spectrum	**A.**	designate
7)	allot	**B.**	unity
8)	rapport	**C.**	range
9)	cohesion	**D.**	compatibility
10)	void	**E.**	abyss

END
of
LESSON 19

Lesson 20

Essay

The optional essay portion of the 2016 SAT allocates 50 minutes to read a short passage and respond with a well-organized analytical essay based on observations of the passage (no opinions or personal experiences—all the information needed to write the essay will be contained within the passage).

Three criteria of the essay will be scored: reading, analysis, and writing. After completing an essay, evaluate your writing using the scoring guide provided on pages 188-189.

Prompt

Reread the passage from **Lesson 13**.

As you read the passage, consider how the author uses the following elements:

- **evidence** – the use of facts, examples, data, research, etc., to support claims
- **reasoning** – the development of ideas and the connection of evidence in support of the argument
- **style** – persuasive language, word choice, emotional appeals, and figurative language that add power to ideas

Write an essay in which you explain how Jefferson builds an argument to persuade his audience that America should engage in changing the way of life of the Native Americans while funding an expedition to the West. In your essay, analyze how the author uses one or more of the elements listed above to strengthen the logic and persuasiveness of his argument. Be sure that your analysis focuses on the most relevant features of the passage.

Your essay should not explain whether you agree with the author's claims, but, rather, how the author builds an argument to persuade his audience.

Essay Scoring Guide*

Points	Reading	Analysis	Writing
4	- demonstrates thorough comprehension of the source text - shows an understanding of the text's central idea(s) and of most important details and how they interrelate, demonstrating a comprehensive understanding of the text - free of errors of fact or interpretation with regard to the text - skillful use of textual evidence (quotations, paraphrases, or both), demonstrating a complete understanding of the source text	- offers an insightful analysis of the source text and demonstrates a sophisticated understanding of the analytical task - offers a thorough, well-considered evaluation of the author's use of evidence, reasoning, stylistic and persuasive elements, and feature(s) of the student's own choosing - contains relevant, sufficient, and strategically chosen support for claim(s) or point(s) made - focuses consistently on those features of the text that are most relevant to addressing the task	- cohesive and demonstrates a highly effective use and command of language - includes a precise central claim - includes a skillful introduction and conclusion - demonstrates a deliberate and highly effective progression of ideas both within paragraphs and throughout the essay - has a wide variety in sentence structures - demonstrates a consistent use of precise word choice; the response maintains a formal style and objective tone. - shows a strong command of the conventions of standard written English and is free or virtually free of errors
3	- demonstrates effective comprehension of the source text - shows an understanding of the text's central idea(s) and important details - free of substantive errors of fact and interpretation with regard to the text - makes appropriate use of textual evidence (quotations, paraphrases, or both), demonstrating an understanding of the source text	- offers an effective analysis of the source text and demonstrates an understanding of the analytical task - competently evaluates the author's use of evidence, reasoning, and/or stylistic and persuasive elements, and/or feature(s) of the student's own choosing - contains relevant and sufficient support for claim(s) or point(s) made - focuses primarily on those features of the text that are most relevant to addressing the task	- is mostly cohesive and demonstrates effective use and control of language - includes a central claim or implicit controlling idea - includes an effective introduction and conclusion; demonstrates a clear progression of ideas both within paragraphs and throughout the essay - includes variety in sentence structures; demonstrates some precise word choice; maintains a formal style and objective tone - shows a good control of the conventions of standard written English and is free of significant errors that detract from the quality of writing

*Adapted from materials appearing on www.collegeboard.com, the official website of the College Board

Essay Scoring Guide continued:

Points	Reading	Analysis	Writing
2	- demonstrates some comprehension of the source text - shows an understanding of the text's central idea(s) but not of important details - may contain errors of fact and/or interpretation with regard to the text - makes limited and/or haphazard use of textual evidence (quotations, paraphrases, or both), demonstrating some understanding of the source text	- offers limited analysis of the source text and demonstrates only partial understanding of the analytical task - identifies and attempts to describe the author's use of evidence, reasoning, and/or stylistic and persuasive elements, and/or feature(s) of the student's own choosing, but merely asserts rather than explains their importance, or one or more aspects of the response's analysis are unwarranted based on the text - contains little or no support for claim(s) or point(s) made - may lack a clear focus on those features of the text that are most relevant to addressing the task	- demonstrates little or no cohesion and limited skill in the use and control of language - may lack a clear central claim or controlling idea, or may deviate from the claim or idea over the course of the response - may include an ineffective introduction and/or conclusion; may demonstrate some progression of ideas within paragraphs but not throughout the response - has limited variety in sentence structures; sentence structures may be repetitive. - demonstrates general or vague word choice; word choice may be repetitive; may deviate noticeably from a formal style and objective tone - shows a limited control of the conventions of standard written English and contains errors that detract from the quality of writing and may impede understanding
1	- demonstrates little or no comprehension of the source text - fails to show an understanding of the text's central idea(s), and may include only details without reference to central idea(s) - may contain numerous errors of fact and/or interpretation with regard to the text - makes little or no use of textual evidence (quotations, paraphrases, or both), demonstrating little or no understanding of the source text	- offers little or no analysis or ineffective analysis of the source text and demonstrates little or no understanding of the analytic task - identifies without explanation some aspects of the author's use of evidence, reasoning, and/or stylistic and persuasive elements, and/or feature(s) of the student's choosing, or numerous aspects of the response's analysis are unwarranted based on the text - contains little or no support for claim(s) or point(s) made, or support is largely irrelevant - may not focus on features of the text that are relevant to addressing the task - offers no discernible analysis (e.g., is largely or exclusively a summary)	- demonstrates little or no cohesion and inadequate skill in the use and control of language - may lack a clear central claim or controlling idea - lacks a recognizable introduction and conclusion; does not have a discernible progression of ideas - lacks variety in sentence structures; sentence structures may be repetitive; demonstrates general and vague word choice; word choice may be poor or inaccurate; may lack a formal style and objective tone - shows a weak control of the conventions of standard written English and may contain numerous errors that undermine the quality of writing

GLOSSARY

Vocabulary Terms

Lesson 1

aspiration	*n.*	a hope, dream, or goal
assimilate	*v.*	to adopt the ideas or culture of another
base	*adj.*	morally low; despicable
contented	*adj.*	satisfied
conviction	*n.*	a strong belief or opinion
haughty	*adj.*	believing oneself to be superior to others
impudence	*n.*	offensiveness and disrespect
Nihilist	*n.*	a person of the belief that life is meaningless and beliefs are pointless
overwrought	*adj.*	tense or agitated
permeate	*v.*	to pass through and spread throughout
perpetual	*adj.*	lasting forever; occurring regularly
propagandist	*n.*	a person who campaigns for or against a specific cause or organization by presenting information most favorable to his or her position
qualm	*n.*	a doubt, fear, or concern
rankled	*v.*	caused resentment and irritation
yearn	*v.*	to have an intense desire for something; to long for something

Lesson 2

accommodate	*v.*	to consider and satisfy the needs of; to make comfortable in a situation
augured	*adj.*	predicted; presumed
bankruptcy	*n.*	the state of official ruin, often financial
gravitate	*v.*	to move or be pulled toward or attracted to something as though by an unseen force
inherently	*adv.*	by nature, from within
obsolete	*adj.*	outdated or no longer useful
plausible	*adj.*	seeming credible or likely
recollect	*v.*	to remember something
resurgence	*n.*	a rebirth in popularity or demand
tactile	*adj.*	pertaining to the sense of touch

Lesson 3

counsel	*n.*	a suggestion or advice
cumberer	*n.*	a hindrance or burden
idleness	*n.*	a state of prolonged inactivity
ignoble	*adj.*	dishonorable or disgraceful
lavish	*v.*	to give in abundance; to bestow generously
preeminently	*adv.*	with superiority to all others
remunerative	*adj.*	profitable; financially rewarding
republic	*n.*	a form of government in which the people hold the power and elect officials to rule within the limits of law or a constitution
slothful	*adj.*	acting sluggish or moving slowly
stern	*adj.*	appearing serious and unyielding
virile	*adj.*	having energetic, masculine qualities

Lesson 4

adverse	*adj.*	opposing or unfavorable
albeit	*conj.*	although
definitive	*adj.*	complete and conclusive; authoritatively final
deleterious	*adj.*	harmful or injurious
dilemma	*n.*	a situation requiring a choice between undesirable options
discard	*v.*	to dispose of; to throw away
leach	*v.*	to percolate or drain through a material
ratify	*v.*	to give formal approval
salvage	*v.*	to rescue or recover goods or property from destruction or loss
saturated	*adj.*	filled to capacity, especially with a liquid
sheath	*n.*	a close-fitting covering, usually for a blade or a tool

Lesson 5

abjure	*v.*	to renounce; to officially reject
aegis	*n.*	protection
antiquated	*adj.*	outdated; useless
arbitrary	*adj.*	random or subjective
aspire	*v.*	to strive toward a goal; to desire strongly
coerce	*v.*	to force someone through threats or intimidation
compel	*v.*	to force to do
concord	*n.*	a peaceful state of agreement or stability
consent	*v.*	to agree; to demonstrate a willingness
contract	*v.*	to agree formally
despotism	*n.*	the use of absolute power
discord	*n.*	disagreement and conflict
equity	*n.*	fairness
evince	*v.*	to demonstrate clearly; to make evident
exasperate	*v.*	to irritate and anger
felicity	*n.*	happiness; good fortune
insurmountable	*adj.*	unable to be overcome; unachievable
licentious	*adj.*	morally unrestrained; ignoring laws or morality
pious	*adj.*	earnestly devout, especially to a religion
posterity	*n.*	future generations
prudent	*adj.*	wise and cautious in judgment
repress	*v.*	to block or to limit
supplication	*n.*	a humble request; a petition
tumult	*n.*	a social uproar or disturbance
tutelary	*adj.*	pertaining to guardianship or protection
tyrant	*n.*	a cruel and unjust ruler
venerable	*adj.*	admired or respected
vindictive	*adj.*	revengeful

SAT Power Prep: Ascend
GLOSSARY

Lesson 6

abstract *adj.* existing only as an idea; conceptual
ad nauseam *adv.* endlessly
anatomical *adj.* pertaining to the structure of a living being
charlatan *n.* a person who fraudulently professes special knowledge or skill; a fraud
debilitating *adj.* causing to weaken or impair
debunk *v.* to expose as false
decipher *v.* to determine the meaning of
disparate *adj.* distinct; fundamentally different
motif *n.* a recurring idea
neuron *n.* a cell within the nervous system
plethora *n.* an overabundance
potential *n.* possible, but not yet reached, capability
rigid *adj.* firmly set; unchanging
tomography *n.* the use of X-rays to view a specific plane at a specific depth within a body
trauma *n.* severe injury or distress

Lesson 7

assertion *n.* a statement or claim
duplicitous *adj.* dishonest; deceitful
hysteria *n.* a state of panic
intimately *adv.* deeply and personally
physiological *adj.* pertaining to how a living being functions
prestige *n.* high standing; honorable reputation
submission *n.* the act of surrendering to the will of another
validity *n.* substance and truthfulness

Lesson 8

attributable *adj.* able to be regarded as having been caused by a specific source or cause
barometric *adj.* related to atmospheric pressure
corrosive *adj.* causing to be deteriorated or eaten away, usually chemically
cumulative *adj.* accumulated; increased from having been added together
deviation *n.* the act of moving away from what is expected
fraught *adj.* filled (with something unwanted)
hull *n.* the greater, outer structure
increment *n.* one of a series of individual increases or gains
latitude *n.* the distance, on Earth, measured north or south of the equator, represented by horizontal lines on a map
longitude *n.* the distance, on Earth, measured east or west of the Prime Meridian, represented by vertical lines on a map
nautical *adj.* pertaining to ships or sailing
persistence *n.* the steadfast drive to complete a purpose or reach a goal in spite of adversity
reckoning *n.* calculating based on estimates
stipulate *v.* to specify a demand as part of an agreement

Lesson 9

connotation *n.* the secondary meaning or the meaning associated with something
derogatory *adj.* disparaging or intentionally offensive
descent *n.* lineage; a derivation from ancestors
dialect *n.* a distinct variation of a standard language, usually used by a specific group or people in a region
reconcile *v.* to reestablish a relationship after a dispute
relevant *adj.* related to the matter at hand
solitude *n.* a state of loneliness or isolation

Lesson 11

adjacent *adj.* having a common boundary; adjoining
annals *n.* recorded history, often as descriptive accounts
compass *v.* to understand or comprehend
confederation *n.* a union for a common purpose
delineate *v.* to portray through drawing or words
immaterial *adj.* irrelevant or unimportant to
incursion *n.* a raid in another's territory
labyrinth *n.* a maze
materially *adv.* substantially; considerably
solemn *adj.* deeply serious
sublime *adj.* grand and inspiring deep respect
tenacious *adj.* stubborn or unwavering
venerable *adj.* worthy of great respect

Lesson 12

affluent *adj.* wealthy
beget *v.* to produce or cause
capitalistic *adj.* pertaining to an economic system in which business is privately owned, and individuals are free to manage their own property
collateral *n.* property offered as a guarantee that a loan will be repaid
destitute *adj.* lacking basic needs; completely impoverished
dividend *n.* a portion of a company's profits paid to shareholders or owners
ensue *v.* to follow or occur as a result
enterprise *n.* a bold undertaking or venture, especially a business
entrepreneur *n.* a person who starts a business
eradicate *v.* to eliminate completely
exploitation *n.* taking advantage of a person or situation
guise *n.* an outward appearance, often false or deceptive
humanitarian *adj.* pertaining to the improvement of human welfare and happiness
Impoverished *adj.* lacking basic needs or income
innovative *adj.* using new or creative methods
mandate *n.* an official order or instruction
portfolio *n.* a group or collection of investments
saturated *adj.* filled to maximum capacity
sector *n.* a distinct part or section
sustain *v.* to support or maintain

GLOSSARY

Lesson 13

accoutrement *n.* equipment other than basic items; an accessory
apparatus *n.* a collection of tools, devices, or equipment
appropriation *n.* funds devoted for a specific use or the act of marking funds for a specific use
capital *adj.* pertaining to financial assets
commerce *n.* the buying and selling of goods and services
continuance *n.* a continuation or lengthening
diminish *v.* to reduce or lessen
diminution *n.* a reduction; a lessening
domestic *adj.* pertaining to the household or family life
dominion *n.* a territory or controlled region
effect *v.* to cause or to make happen
endeavor *v.* to try with considerable effort
expedient *adj.* suitable for the situation; appropriate
gratification *n.* a source of satisfaction; a pleasure
intercourse *n.* interaction and communication between people
peltry *n.* animal skins, processed or unprocessed
portage *n.* a route or track, usually used for transporting goods or traveling
principal *adj.* most important
principle *n.* a rule or policy
sanction *n.* official approval
uncultivated *adj.* (1) not prepared for use as farmland (2) lacking knowledge and social skills

Lesson 14

aerobics *n.* exercise that works the heart and lungs
autonomic *adj.* occurring spontaneously, without thought; involuntary
cortex *n.* the outer, protective layer of a bodily organ
deprivation *n.* a deficiency of something essential
deterioration *n.* a decline in quality or character
haphazardly *adv.* at random
incite *v.* to provoke or instigate
lethargy *n.* drowsiness; a state of lacking energy
nucleus *n.* an essential, central part; a core
ominous *adj.* threatening
phenomenon *n.* an unusual occurrence
primeval *adj.* having existed in the earliest stage or time
reticular *adj.* resembling a network or net-like form

Lesson 15

aerosolized *adj.* turned into fine particles
catalyst *n.* a person or thing that causes a process or an event to happen
catastrophic *adj.* having a sudden, widespread, and disastrous effect
eponymous *adj.* named after a particular person or thing
flagellum *n.* a cell appendage like a tail, usually used for propulsion
formidable *adj.* inspiring fear or dread

Lesson 15 continued

gangrene *n.* the death and subsequent decay of body tissue
macrophage *n.* a large, white blood cell that fights infection in the body
medieval *adj.* pertaining to the Middle Ages; extremely old-fashioned
menace *n.* a serious threat
pandemic *n.* an outbreak of disease over a wide geographical area
pneumonic *adj.* pertaining to the lungs
propagation *n.* the act of multiplying or increasing in number
retribution *n.* punishment for wrongdoing
scapegoat *v.* to make someone else bear the blame for others
stave *v.* to fight off or repel
subsequent *adj.* following in order; occurring after
unimpeded *adj.* not slowed or hindered
vector *n.* the source or carrier of a disease

Lesson 16

contemporary *adj.* modern or current
curtail *v.* to cut short or reduce
exclusivity *n.* the state of being limited or accessible to only a select few
fluorescent *adj.* pertaining to the generation of light by electrifying gas (versus the heating of an element)
font *n.* written letters and numbers having a unique size and shape, usually as a subdivision of a typeface
manipulate *v.* to manage or make changes to
nuance *n.* a subtle difference
salary *n.* regular wages in return for services
substantial *adj.* of considerable size
superfluous *adj.* exceeding what is necessary
typeface *n.* a collection of fonts that share the same basic design

Lesson 17

actualize *v.* to make real
candid *adj.* informal and unplanned
caption *n.* an explanation accompanying a photograph
empathetic *adj.* imagining and trying to understand the feelings of another
haven *n.* a safe place
philanthropy *n.* charity work
unobtrusive *adj.* modest; not stealing attention
vibrant *adj.* giving the impression of having energy or activity

SAT Power Prep: Ascend

GLOSSARY

Lesson 18

aquifer	*n.*	an underground rock layer that holds water
depletion	*n.*	a reduction or exhaustion
detrimental	*adj.*	seriously harmful
exacerbate	*v.*	to make worse
hydrologist	*n.*	a scientist who studies the effects of water on and throughout the earth
inevitability	*n.*	unavoidability; impossibility of preventing
overdraft	*n.*	the taking or withdrawing of too much of something
subsidence	*n.*	a sinking or settling

Lesson 19

allot	*v.*	to distribute in portions
anonymous	*adj.*	of unknown identity
anthropologist	*n.*	a person who studies human society and culture
autonomy	*n.*	independence
cohesion	*n.*	togetherness
discordant	*adj.*	lacking harmony
mitigate	*v.*	to make less severe or damaging
rapport	*n.*	a relationship dependent on understanding and trust
sever	*v.*	to cut off or separate from the whole
spectrum	*n.*	the whole range
void	*n.*	emptiness; abyss